Agile

Exposed

Agile
Exposed

Blowing the whistle on Agile hype.
An overview of Agile, where it came from
and the principles that make it work.

by
Barry Evans
MBCS CEng CITP

Author of The Trousers of Reality

www.TrousersOfReality.com

Code Green Publishing
Coventry, UK

Copyright © 2011 by Barry Evans

ISBN 978-1-907215-17-9

All illustrations by the Author unless otherwise stated
Cover design by Code Green Publishing
Back cover photo of Author by Richard Hadley

Version 1.1

Published by Code Green Publishing
www.codegreenpublishing.com

For my brother Jamie.
A truly talented and generous man.

Table of Contents

Part One - Agile Examined

Part Two – Agile Analysed

Part Three – Software Development Project Models

Part Four – Observations and Advice

"Without ambition one starts nothing. Without work one finishes nothing. The prize will not be sent to you. You have to win it. The man who knows how will always have a job. The man who also knows why will always be his boss. As to methods there may be a million and then some, but principles are few. The man who grasps principles can successfully select his own methods. The man who tries methods, ignoring principles, is sure to have trouble."

Ralph Waldo Emerson

Part One - Agile Examined

Introduction

Having been involved in software development and Agile since the 1990's as a programmer and then a manager and coach, I am saddened that programmers and their managers have been convinced to miss the point as increasingly cynical attempts to commoditise and "cash in" turn Agile into a dirty word. No matter what the packaging-over-content gurus and the marketing people say, the principles and ideas behind Agile are still relevant and necessary. Agile, as practised by those who made it work, was not about sound-bytes, the feel-good factor, groovy techniques, avoiding documentation, cutting corners or dumbing down a profession. It is about encouraging solid programming skills based on good code design and it is focussed on harnessing technology, experience and expertise to make something that has maximum and enduring usefulness to the end user.

So what happened?

Agile Hype

Hype is short for hyperbole and hypodermic. Hype, in the sense of hyperbole, is a description that is exaggerated intentionally. Hyped up, in the sense of hypodermic, a tool used to deliver drugs into the system, is to create a false sense of confidence. These days the meaning of hype is very closely related to the public relations term spin, the art of distorting interpretation of events to suit specific ends – a form of disingenuous and manipulative propaganda that ignores anything that does not support the desired position.

There is a lot of both hype and spin associated with Agile. Some of it is intentional but most of it derives from wilful ignorance. It is carried out by individuals, organisations and entire methodologies who want to claim the benefits without doing the hard work. In many cases these can be found trying to extend the Agile Honeymoon and disappear when the savings have been spent. Agile works initially for these people because your organisation   has had some responsible people there who have put you in credit.

The claims that Agile will allow you do deliver more, faster, cheaper and with fewer people is both spin and hype. There are elements of truth to this interpretation but they ignore much of the reality that underlines this statement and the consequences and requirements of achieving these things.

In software development all of the benefits of Agile rely primarily on a well structured code base and then on a relationship of trust between the management and the production layers of the organisation. Neither of these things happens magically just because you start to talk about Agile or prioritise requirements. The law of conservation of energy applies and you will get these things when you have put the effort into building the foundations required and maintaining them. This applies equally to the code and to the relationships within the organisation.

You also need to examine the terms "more", "cheaper", "faster" and "fewer people" with the law of conservation of energy in mind. The law of conservation of energy is this – energy can neither be created nor destroyed, it can only be transformed from one state to another – therefore the sum of all energy in a system is constant. It is the underlying principle of the universe. With it at my back I can promise you that Agile will not allow you to get something for nothing. It will not magically create bug free systems. That takes effort and energy. With this law at my back I can promise you that there are ways of applying deep principles, and you can call them Agile or whatever you like, that will allow you to direct the energy you have at your disposal toward real and lasting value.

- You will still need all the people required to construct a maintainable and functional system. Fewer of them will be involved in systems maintenance and more of them will be involved in productive work.
- To do things properly will still take the time it takes.
- Deliveries will be produced faster but their quality will still depend on the skill of the programmers and the foundations you encourage and allow them to put in place.
- You will have the same amount of work to do but more of it will be useful to you in the here and now.
- Finally the law of conservation of energy ultimately means that you get what you pay for. What Agile does better than anything else when properly applied is to identify failure quickly. It makes it harder to keep pushing ahead on a doomed project. That is money in the bank for a responsible organisation.

Agile — The elephant in the boardroom

"One morning I shot an elephant in my pyjamas.
How he got in my pyjamas I'll never know."
— Groucho Marx

We often describe something obvious that no one wants to discuss and which is deliberately and studiously ignored as "the elephant in the room". We also use this phrase to describe an obvious solution to a controversial problem that no one will discuss for fear it will be embarrassing or will throw up some uncomfortable facts.

If there is an elephant in the room and you want to describe it to someone on the other side of the table who has their back turned to it and refuses to turn around, you have to do several things.

- Describe what you are looking at.
- Explain how it got there.
- Deal with other people on your side of the table who are trying to pretend that the elephant is a gorilla smoking a cigar.
- Explore the consequences of having an elephant present.
- Interest the person enough to make them turn around.

When describing elephants we get into some tricky territory about perception, categorisation and communication.

When most people, not including Antoine de Saint Exupery[1], are asked to draw an elephant, they are likely to draw something like this:

What makes this picture represent an elephant? What tips you off? The ears? The toenails? The trunk?

This is a trick question because none of those things is in this picture. It is a line on paper, which seeks to define how an elephant would appear in space. It relies on you having seen an elephant, something like an elephant or a much more convincing representation of an elephant at some previous time.

While that is all very interesting the real question is what is the line really doing? My proposal is that it can do nothing more than try to define the outline of an elephant. It defines the boundaries of an elephant. In describing anything, we have to decide where that thing starts being itself and where it stops being itself. We have to define its boundaries.

---

1   He drew something that looked like a hat which turned out to be a boa constrictor that had just ingested an elephant.

If I just showed you this:

Which is the bit inside the elephant here:

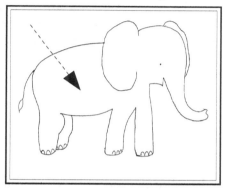

Although it is well within the boundaries of the elephant, it would not be very helpful. A helpful picture of an elephant would:

- Describe where the elephant stops being an elephant so that you can get some idea of its shape and features and of the space it occupies.
- Establish common points of reference that would allow you to visualise the elephant – perhaps a rhino or an anteater.
- Set a real world scale once you have the shape, category and general features in mind.

Even the most detailed picture by the most proficient artist has to define where the elephant stops being an elephant. To do this the artist will most probably draw just the outer skin of the elephant. If you saw a picture of the elephant's heart or lungs, which are essential to the existence of the elephant, you would have no idea of the concept of the elephant except that it is probably a big, air breathing living being.

Although I understand that many readers would expect me to set about exposing Agile by giving them a detailed description of pair programming, test first, user stories and all the other Agile paraphernalia and how they fit together, I am not going to. This would be the equivalent of either showing you this as an elephant:

Or of parading its internal organs in front of you and asking you to guess what it looks like and expecting you to know how to ride one.

"Why" do Agile is more important than "How" to do Agile. A true understanding of "Why" you are doing something ensures that your actions are consistent with and supportive of your desired outcomes. If you concentrate solely on how to do something, actions can easily become perverted and evolve away from your purpose. Knowing how is essential but it should always be preceded by understanding why. When you understand "why" you can define the boundaries and discern the best "how to's". This is the heart of what works in Agile. How we build the rest depends on environment and skill.

Elephant is a term for a large mammal with a trunk and big ears. There are three species: two in Africa and one in India. Once you have seen one you will never forget it and neither, legend goes, will it forget you.

Agile is an umbrella term for a set of lightweight processes mostly used in software development. Once you have been part of a genuine Agile project you will want to repeat the experience. Agile is more a philosophy, an honest enquiry and an approach than a set of rules or techniques. It deals with the reality of change. Although the techniques sometimes appear to work independently of their body, more often they can be only as useful as ground elephant tusk is as an aphrodisiac. Tusks make more sense on the elephant and Agile techniques make more sense as part of an ongoing Agile outcome.

People sometimes talk convincingly about pink elephants in relation to the effects of alcohol; and white elephants in relation to the effects of foolish spending. There are anthropomorphic cartoon elephants and cuddly stuffed toy elephants. While these can be diverting and even useful in their context, they are products of the imagination and they do not help you to understand the essential nature of actual elephants. The same can be said of many of the products of fevered marketing imaginations that seek to sell you Agile.

Many of these products have blurred the boundaries of Agile making it very difficult to make out its actual nature. In exposing Agile we must look for boundaries. In this book I will look at the history of Agile and the problems it sought to address, just as I would describe the African plains and the Indian jungles to put elephants in perspective. I will also unmask some cardboard replicas of Agile which are like cartoon elephants that have no heart or lungs, merely the shell of a shape.

The Outline of Agile

We can start to see the outline of Agile through its outcomes[2]. The outcomes of Agile are:

1 Harness the power of collaborative working, consensus and valuable skills.
2 Produce maintainable systems that can handle changes, fixes and new requirements effectively and efficiently.
3 Establish a direct connection between the capabilities of the technology and the needs of the stakeholders and customers.
4 Focus on what the user community is actually doing with the system so that expensive and valuable effort is not wasted on functionality that will rarely or never be used and will be directed toward the production of valuable and useful business tools.

If techniques and practices achieve this then they are Agile. You will achieve flexibility of response and a calibration of business priority and technical reality. Everything else is smoke and mirrors.

---

2   This is expressed in the Agile manifesto as Agile values:
   1. Individuals and interactions over processes and tools.
   2. Working software over comprehensive documentation.
   3. Customer collaboration over contract negotiation.
   4. Responding to change over following a plan.

Looking to history for illumination

Bosses and workers

Agile began with a group of programmers trying to deal with a pandemic of misunderstanding about their profession in a hierarchical business and career model inherited from the worst interpretation of capitalism. This interpretation was a hangover from the industrial revolution.

During the industrial revolution you had bosses and workers. Workers provided brawn and bosses provided brain. Anyone with brains became a boss.

At least that was the theory.

In practice commerce has always depended on skilled workers and they have always been underrated. It is easier to create a kind of caste system that contains an underclass that can be considered disposable and made to doubt their value than to admit the dependency that wealth creation has on skill and experience.

A mill worker during the industrial revolution had skills to work the mill machinery to manufacture products. Once established these skill-sets changed slowly so they could be captured in the instruction manual for the machinery and the processes and habits of the mill. They could be bound to the mill and the machinery. In this way workers could be as mass produced as the products and thus easily controlled and devalued.

In the information age we can think of computer programmers as modern day mill workers in the IT industry. In the analogy it is tempting to think of the computer hardware as the mill but that would be to completely misunderstand the nature of information technology. In reality the computer is more akin to a tool-belt or overalls that the industrial revolution worker carried from place to place. This is especially relevant with the ubiquitous nature of modern communications networks. The programmer's mind is the mill that shapes and transforms basic materials into valuable products that manage the increasingly complex information flow of our businesses and societies. This product cannot be as easily defined as a manufactured product — because the product is change itself. Programming is the art of mapping change.

Over twenty years ago a wise old marketing director for a successful IT company confided in me over a beer that even the best computer systems have a useful life of between *three* and *five* years. Understanding this is fundamental to making decisions about how much to invest and where to invest it in IT. Everything I have ever seen in my career bears out this nugget of wisdom. People who do not know or accept this find themselves constantly at odds with and frustrated by IT. What I have also discovered through a lifetime working with computer systems is that even during their short shelf life systems have to be tended if you want them to work for you in real world environments. Future-proofing by attempting to define future requirements in detail and adding them to systems is a waste of time, resource and sanity. Implementing requirements that are not going to be immediately used gets in the way of those that you want to use right now. Unused, speculative and ill conceived functionality and requirements will make it much more difficult to implement useful functionality in the future when you actually understand what it is you really need.

You can accept that a gardener's job is not finished when the flowers have been planted, the water feature installed and the grass trimmed. However well you may think you have planned your garden you know that weather, the tendency of green things to grow and the need to weed means you need to keep gardening. You cannot cut next years grass this autumn and putting down weed killer or Agent Orange to keep it from growing sort of destroys the purpose of a lawn in the first place. You need a gardener that can do things when they need to be done and when they can be done.

While we can understand how many businesses want to go back to the good old days of cheap indentured labour, we are evolving. The programmer is a philosopher and designer who works with esoteric concepts such as the nature of logic. The programmer cannot work from a manual because progress accelerates at such a pace that the manual would be outdated before it could be completed.

The world moves on and with it the nature of business. Knowledge workers do not manufacture commodities you can sell independently — they are bound to their product. Their ability to work with knowledge is their commodity. I examine this in more detail in the second volume of the Trousers of Reality — Managing Knowledge. No matter how much some businesses would like it to be, these are workers whose value is becoming apparent to themselves. Off-shoring, outsourcing, detailed, impossible methodologies and psychological chicanery are being trialled as ways to make the worker disposable again. Because of the speed of response, the complexity of function and ease of use that the marketplace demands we can see the folly of this all around us. These things offer up misdirection and hide consequences. They are no substitutes for experience, judgement and dedication.

Agile at its best recognises realities of the information age and the need to ally power to skill, vision to ability, and the theory to the practice.

What changed?

Computers have become the bedrock upon which all business in the modern world is carried out. They were initially a toy and a curiosity but somewhere along the line they became ubiquitous and necessary. As this became clear, it was expected by many commentators, futurologists and business analysts that if the computing fad persisted, programming them would become easier as they became more user friendly.

They were right but not in the way they meant. They could not have been expected to really understand where computer science and business would want to take them. It is easier to code computers today than it has ever been. Being a computer programmer is also more difficult and requires more knowledge and skill today than ever before. This paradox looks likely to deepen and persist.

Easier but harder coding

Well think about computer games of 20 or even 10 years ago. Now have a quick search through the monthly releases of games available. The older games look like stone age cave paintings beside the explosion of renaissance skill unleashed by the demand and the expanding possibilities of the medium. The sheer complexity of modern games is staggering. What customers expect has exponentially exploded into creativity and technical skill that would make programming those early games child's play with modern tools and computer languages. It is a bit like saying that modern cars go faster than model T Fords therefore we should spend less time travelling. We spend more time than ever in our cars and sometimes not going as far. Expectations and environments change.

This same sort of thing happened with business computing except even more so. The problem is that in business there is less appreciation for the artistry involved in making computers work. There is a presupposition that because computer code is based on mathematics, that programming them should be just a matter of feeding developers the right set of instructions to translate into the languages that they use to talk to computers.

Initially people who start programming get very excited about how easy it is to construct syntactically and semantically correct code. As they progress they soon find that this is also a problem. Computers do what you tell them to do. Exactly what you tell them to do, nothing more. Add in half a million transactions a second, inconsistent data, tens or thousands of people using the application in ways that you could never have guessed at, insert it into a fragile environment made up of other programs written by lunatics from history and you might start to get a glimpse of the skill Programmers need in their profession.

Throw customers, bosses and stakeholders into the mix who think they understand what programmers do and try to instruct and second guess them with limited pigeon "*computerese*" rather than just tell them what it is that they really want. It is a bit like going to a mechanic with a faulty carburettor that you have diagnosed as a spark plug problem while insisting that the windscreen wiper mechanism houses the spark plugs. Imagine if you started to tell the mechanic that your requirements were to unscrew that bit there (pointing at the wiper mechanism) and insert some new spark plugs and insisting that when the mechanic starts talking about windscreen wipers, spark plugs and carburettors that they are deliberately trying to blind you with jargon, introduce unnecessary work and are unprofessional because they are unwilling to simply do what you ask.

This is the kind of surreal position in which programmers often find themselves.

The logical but insane response

Well, if you are a programmer, you decide that trying to educate the customer in the details and intricacies is a waste of time. By the time you get them to the stage that they have the requisite technical skill to fully understand, they will have effected a lengthy and costly career change and there will be a new rash of managers and customers queuing up with spark plug instructions. You need some way to simplify the communication process. You need some way to get them to tell you what they want and to stop telling you how and what they think you should do.

This is the half of the story that well intentioned non programmers understand and sell as Agile. They think that this is the whole story and, like the original customers, they make the huge assumption that once you have told the programmer clearly what you want that they will easily translate this into a series of code instructions and deliver it. There is a dangerous myth that programmers do nothing but translate well documented requirements directly into a language the computer will understand. If only it were that easy! Spark plugs and windscreen wipers can be clearly documented as being in the same UML box (UML is a design documentation tool that is lethal in the hands of many non programming designers.)

The other half of the story is of the nature of code. Despite many well intentioned metaphors, creating computer code is neither like building a bridge, building a house nor steering a ship. It is, however, exactly like creating computer code — and we are still finding out what that is like. Nothing like it has ever been done in the history of the world and it is changing rapidly every single day.

Requirements evolution

What we do know is that good code is a fluid and malleable medium that supports change as requirements evolve. Requirements capture is a misnomer. It implies a finality that exists in very few system domains. I propose that requirements evolution is a much more helpful term. This means that good code is never finished. This has long been treated as a fault in the profession but, in fact, it is its strength. Good code evolves with its users and has stages of stability during that evolution called delivery. Your programmers are not just the manufacturers of your system; they are part of it and part of its running cost. You dispose of them at great risk. Many companies are facing this through the stages of grief — denial, anger, bargaining, depression and acceptance:

- Denial:
  - *"Computing is not part of our core business!"*

- — Yes it is. We are in the Information Age. You need IT to survive.
- Anger:
  - *"Well then, let's get some command and control processes to make them do what we tell them to!"*
    - — Spark plugs and windscreen wipers!
- Bargaining:
    - *"Off-shoring and outsourcing will let us contain it and push down the price. Let's use that bargain bin Agile ointment while we are at it!"*
      - — Sorry, because of the nature of systems you will quickly find yourself over a barrel[3] or dealing with systems that don't work or whose maintenance is impossible.
- Depression:
  - *"I hate all nerds, geeks and technophiles — these people are holding me to ransom!"*
    - — Have a look in your IT department — you might have to redefine nerd, geek and technophile to mean smart, socially aware, educated and cooperative youth working with experienced and wise middle age. They are usually pretty commercially aware and realise that their success is tied to yours.
- Acceptance:
  - *"Okay then. Let's move with the times, admit they are highly skilled and that we need them; tell them what we want and accept that you gets what you pays for."*
    - — That's the style.

---

3   External companies controlling your critical information flow will not be slow to lever this advantage.

If this frightens you then don't panic. Remember it is not manufacturing and because of this there are bogeymen we can banish by turning on the light of knowledge.

Deus ex machina

There is one consistency that programmers count on that is totally independent of language and that consistency is the nature of code:

Code is cheap to change. There is a well established myth out there about scales of cost of changing requirements from design to live running.

The myth is convincing and comes with an honest looking diagram like this:

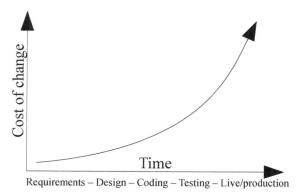

Requirements – Design – Coding – Testing – Live/production

This analysis may look logical but it is false. It is based on ideas from manufacturing. Software development is not manufacturing. In fact many problems arise only when you try to treat software development as if it were manufacturing. The cost of changing the code is not the same as the cost of reengineering a bridge or a house or a car — for which the above would be true. This is only the cost of "*the process*" which surrounds changing the code when software development is treated as a manufacturing exercise. Good code is made to be changed – but we will come to that later. Remember it is all virtual – unlike a house, a bridge or a ship. When you want to get at the foundations of a house or change the way a bridge is anchored to a bank, you have to demolish the whole structure to get at it.

The code bridge will hover in the air over the canyon while you change the posts it is anchored to or even the size and strength of it. You can hold the code house in the air with your pinkie (or version control software) while you re-dig the foundations and add a whole new wing.

The cost of changing well designed code (I mean the structure of the code as designed by professional coders here) looks more like this:

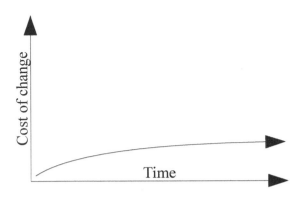

There is a much more gradual increase caused only by the amount of code involved rather than by the difficulty of changing it. It works like this when you recognise that coding is not manufacturing and that the design, the coding and the testing are the same thing and should be dealt with by the same sorts of people.

The programmer began as an analyst-programmer before the functions were separated out in an attempt to model systems development on manufacturing.

What many methodologies regard as design is not systems design; it is a form of detailed and deranged requirements capture about virtual spark plugs and wiper fluid.

The industry recognises that the best testers are always recruited from the best coders and when I was studying management, the received wisdom was to put your **best** programmer on the test team. Testing is not part of the final delivery process — it is part of the essential development process. Good testers make good programmers and good programmers make good testers.

Agile is a view that coding then testing might very well be the horse before the cart in manufacturing but in software development testing is the engine in the race-car.

Good code is elegant and abides to the rules of **high cohesion** (like with like) and **low coupling** (dependencies are kept to an absolute minimum). This is an old idea. Agile developers will tell you that when the bullshit is cleared it is the purpose of almost all of the Agile development techniques to recognise the mercurial nature of code and the need to keep adjusting it. This means that you need to:

- Create code that is easy to change where changes can be isolated and tested.
- Ensure that everyone's skill levels are sufficiently high to maintain this maintainability.

My lessons in Agility

The joy of programming

I first came across Agile principles before the term Agile had been coined. Many of them were the natural lessons I learned from being a professional programmer.

I had fallen in love with programming whilst doing another job altogether. I spent hours programming spreadsheets and databases in my own time and was bitten hard enough by the computing bug to retrain as a software engineer in my mid twenties.

I began my new career in software development in 1991 and I was lucky enough to work with some very professional and skilled programmers. They taught me to respect the basics of good programming.

My first job as a programmer was in an organisation that sent an engineer and a salesperson on all sales visits to potential customers. The engineer was empowered to ensure that the salesperson stuck to the truth and did not exaggerate or oversell the product. The engineer's role at these meetings was to assess the technical feasibility of customer requirements at the first point of contact. If the engineer thought that the software product could not be extended to meet the customer's requirements, the customer was to be told straight away. This led to an environment of trust between clients, salespeople and engineers:

- Feasible and possible technical solutions could be proposed by the engineers at the point of contact with the customers.
- We always delivered because the customer was never promised anything that could not be delivered.

- The technical team were never tied up trying to produce white elephants and therefore they could concentrate on profitable work.
- The technical team became very connected with how customers were using the software and what they really wanted. They became masters of requirements capture and comprehension.
- Customers with whom a particular instance did not produce any work were impressed by the advice and honesty of the company. They almost always came back later. This approach produced more sales in the long run and resulted in the company becoming the fastest growing in its niche.
- Interdepartmental conflict and rivalry were avoided and were replaced with comradeship and professional respect.
- It short circuited the Chinese whisper effect on requirements.
- The sales people learned more about the product they were selling through contact with the technical people and very rarely needed to be overruled.

In short the commercial/IT partnership was a huge success.

Other aspects of pre-Agile I encountered while working for this company were *Pair Programming* and *test driven development*. These concepts had yet to be defined but had emerged as a natural way of working in this company.

When I left this job I found that the lessons I had learned about customers and sales allowed me to progress into technical lead positions elsewhere.

Same planet, different worlds

As I progressed through my career – working for various organisations in a variety of environments – I began to notice that some companies had a strange and distant relationship with their IT departments. I identified some problems with this:

Self writing systems

An egregious idea had emerged that you could generate code directly from designs and that developers would soon be redundant leaving only a need for business analysts. Although this was science fiction it encouraged companies to buy Integrated Development Environments (IDE's) and Computer Aided Software Engineering (CASE) tools including things that purported to allow you to draw pictures of the software you wanted your programmers to code. It was promised that these would soon be able to generate the code without the developers.

Divide and conquer

To prepare for this (happy day for some), software developers (previously analyst/programmers) were split into Software Designers and Software Engineers. Design departments dealt with logical models of the systems and rarely sought the professional input of programmers to their designs. This meant that designs and the actual code went down diverging paths. Programmers had to pretend to follow impractical detailed design documents while actually redesigning something that had a chance of running on a real machine. Many of the paper designs were unworkable because they were written by people recruited for their understanding of the business model and who knew how to work design generation software but did not understand the nature of code or actual computers.

Separation of design from implementation

As designers began to care very little about how requirements were to be physically implemented or even if they could be implemented, it became increasingly difficult for programmers to map requirements onto the actual code bases. It became impossible to explain the difficulty, since the logical model, no matter how infeasible, seemed very logical to those in charge who neither understood code nor saw the need to know about code.

Delivering requirements

As coding increasingly came to be considered a necessary evil on projects, everyone began to talk about *delivering requirements.* This was, and still is, an avoidance of recognising that the end product is code. If the code does not work, it does not matter how many requirements you have signed off. Programmers were often seen as unhelpful and obstructive because of problems they had implementing woolly requirements. The real game should always be to understand actual outcomes and to make sure that the technological capabilities match the expectations. If they don't match, it is the expectations that need to change until technology can deliver what you want for the price you are willing to pay. Until then coding is the art of the possible and you cannot turn it into wish-craft.

Rogue developers

Some programmers, freed from design, high on technology and the cult of the nerd, began to have strange notions about having to work in secret on insanely convoluted code that only they could understand. I am still not sure if they really thought they were "boy wonders" or if they were seeking to ensure their continued employment by trying to be indispensable. Although less experienced programmers often held these guys in awe, well trained programmers had to clean up their code once their game was rumbled and they were ejected from the premises.

Some business people reacted rationally and objected to being held to ransom by these boy-men. Unfortunately many were convinced by the act and thought that this behaviour indicated a genius programmer. The myth still lives on in some environments but the truly great programmers and project managers I have encountered agree that cryptic, unmaintainable code, no matter how clever, is a liability and the sign of an amateur.

Sunday drivers

As programming became devalued some companies were taking people from specialist areas, sending them on a two week training course and then setting them coding. Again the result was bug ridden and unmaintainable code that resembled spaghetti. More experienced programmers had a difficult time trying to explain to their managers that although the code appeared to be working it was a time bomb waiting to go off. Managers were seeing lots of code produced quickly by cheaper, less skilled people[4], while more

---

4   This problem has been brought right up to date with the use of cheap outsourced or off-shored labour because output is not measured in terms of maintainability but in short term project delivery of systems held together with spit and packaging.

expensive programmers were grumbling and taking ages over what appeared to be a few small repairs. What were managers supposed to think?

Lack of interest in the profession leads to lack of respect and trust

Programmers were seen as an amorphous tribe of plug and play equals regardless of their skill, experience and background. It is not difficult to understand why developers began to be perceived as a problem.

The industry as a whole began to suspect that lack of control was the issue. Companies were quick to latch on to this as a reason to introduce even more restrictive command and control measures to anyone involved in software development whether they had been part of the problem or not.

Ivory towers

In the past I know that some IT departments in large companies had certainly held themselves aloof from the business and had tried to create an aura of high priests to a greater calling. Nowadays most IT people have a morbid fear of being accused of being in an ivory tower separated from the real concerns of the business. Many have overcompensated and have fallen into the trap of not holding their own profession in high enough esteem.

Business listening to the wrong advice

In the midst of all this the majority of programmers were skilled craftsmen and craftswomen struggling to keep pace with technology and expectations being set by sales and marketing divisions of large companies. The trouble was and still is that budget holders and managers listen to the salesmen whose job it is to sell dreams and not to the engineers whose job it is to provide practical solutions.

(If this were a documentary I would cue footage of the challenger disaster, the BP oil spill of 2010 and a montage of other high profile cases that represent the tip of the iceberg of the consequences of listening to the sales/middle-management patter rather than the concerns of the engineers.)

There is a basic flaw[5] in a hierarchical communication model which prevents vital information being presented. Because of this the chimera of easy profit has been put ahead of sustainability meaning that anything that did not reduce cost was not discussed. (See page 63 "Cost – Time – Scope"). At the same time, engineers were not vigorous enough in alerting Business to the consequences. They seemed to think that management was another planet and none of their concern, although business outcomes have a direct effect on them.

In reality, professional engineers and programmers are the guides and trackers for business into the uncharted forests of Technology.

The beginnings of outsourcing and off-shoring

In the mid nineties as the craft of coding was falling into disrepute I read Edward Yourdon's "The Decline and Fall of The American Programmer". This was written at the beginning of the nineties and in it he

---

5   People considered to be lower down the model are frequently asked the equivalent of "Have you stopped beating your wife yet?" in a system that only permits them to answer the equivalent of yes or no, both of which are incriminating, rather than inviting them to present pertinent and useful information.

predicted that software could be produced to a higher quality more cheaply in countries like India and Japan. He predicted off-shoring and encouraged more of science fiction's automated code generators to counter it. I did not agree that either off-shoring or undermining systems development as a human based skill was a good idea, but I feared that industry and commerce were going to adopt both. They did and the consequences have not been good. It seems that business stakeholders have been encouraged to understand the role of programmers and the skills involved in systems development less and less. While large tools vendors laugh all the way to offshore banks essential IT becomes more of a liability to the people who, in the name of cost cutting, gave away the essential control that skilled in-house programmers would have provided them with.

Extreme measures

At this time I was also discovering Kent Beck's ideas, later published as Extreme Programming (XP). He proposed that the things that programmers know to be basic principles should be brought to their logical and "extreme" conclusion. These "seditious" ideas included testing, collaboration, modularity, clarity, readable code, understanding the business and client domains, integrating everyone's code more frequently, testing consistency and sharing standards and best practices.

Early adoption of extreme programming

I met other programmers who saw the wisdom in this and we started using these techniques – most notably the idea of test-first which started to address long standing design and maintenance issues.

Test first development

This involved writing automated tests to represent the requirements before we coded the requirements themselves. We found that it was a faster way to produce functionality because it resulted in less speculative code and a much better understanding of the actual requirements. Vague and impossible requirements were identified and transmogrified to something understood and achievable. Code was modularised and its basic structural integrity tested incrementally as it was built. These strong foundations gave us the confidence and ability to build dependable and maintainable functionality.

Continuous integration

It is funny how integration and delivery can be stressful and hateful events of recrimination and blame rather than opportunities to celebrate the skill and hard work that has gone into the system.

When you develop any code, even if you are doing it all on your own, you quickly realise that getting things to work in isolation is the easy part. As soon as you start assembling the pieces you realise how much has been assumed, misunderstood and miscommunicated. Any requirement, design or coding issues, which have been lurking beneath the placid surface of the project, suddenly leap out and attack.

If integration is left until a lot of code has been written, the pressure to deliver, along with defensiveness, fatigue and the weight of the written code, make it all but impossible to do anything but implement quick and dirty fixes and hasty patches to paper over the cracks.

It is not just for this delivery or this integration. All subsequent deliveries will see these problems festering and getting progressively worse.

It is better to discover conflicts and design errors before coding and design dependencies start to gather around them.

In order to make delivery less stressful, we quickly learned to steal time to do integrations during development. We were able to expose dependencies and design issues. We were able to test the structural integrity of the whole edifice. We were able to examine how different parts of the whole solution affect each other and use this information to guide ongoing design and architecture decisions.

Earlier and more frequent integration also has the effect of slowing down and educating some of the more gung-ho. It encourages people to take more care because the consequences are more immediate. This apparent slowing of immediate progress to speed up overall progress is only counter intuitive until you have been through the integration and delivery of a complex system.

Customer collaboration

We identified key customers and invited them to try early version of the code to check that what we were doing matched their expectations. We found that customers were able to be clearer about what they wanted when they could see what the system looked like on a monitor. We found we were delivering software that might not have matched the initial design documents but that did provide more of the functionality that customers needed. Really clued in customers then fed these new requirements through the design departments which had no idea that they were giving us change requests that had already been implemented. Customers and programmers had begun working together as a team.

Pair programming

Project managers often wanted to parcel the system up into easy to manage work packages rather than easy to implement chunks of the system. The goal was often to make people "responsible" in a blame culture that prepared for project failure under managers who wanted to be sure they had someone to shove into the firing line. Programmers could often find themselves coding parts of a system that only really fitted together on paper. The situations we were trying to avoid were:

1. A system that did not integrate when the parts were brought together for the first time at delivery. This was and still is the major cause of project over run.
2. Some poor devil left holding an impossible technical task with all sorts of dangling requirements and dependencies.
3. Nobody knowing what anybody else's code was doing, how it was structured nor whether anybody else would be able to understand or make changes to it.

Working together in groups with regular code reviews, voluntary standards and integration exercises, using stubs and drivers that later evolved into mock objects, we secretly undermined the process directives and delivered the software customers wanted. We produced code that was maintainable and that could take new requirements without major redesigns. Management soon noticed that we were outperforming other projects and wanted to know what we were doing. What we were doing proved to be too simple for most managers used to a diet of expensive tools and complex solutions that could be used to impress their own managers and justify the enormous outlays already made.

Agile formula for success

In marched the "*scale it up*" brigade and the enterprise tools vendors. In marched the "*this can be documented, de-skilled, downsized, certified, scaled up, bottled and painted any colour you want for a price*" gang. Programmers had worked long and hard to have Agile recognised as a legitimate way to approach code and now it was being used as a formula to control them.

Turning software development into a formula is exactly the false hope that many vendors, methodologists and other assorted screw-balls have packaged and stamped with Agile for rather gullible clients. Regardless of how much it would calm project offices and budget holders around the world, something as complex as programming cannot be turned into a formula.

Deploying Agile does not make any of the necessary components any cheaper – it makes the project as a whole cheaper by making sure you only invest in the necessary components. It makes project investment as a whole less risky by exposing projects that are going to fail and projects that have been oversold, underestimated, under funded or otherwise had their implementation reality twisted for a variety of reasons. It does this early in the life of the project and thereby saves the money and effort that would otherwise have been spent on impossible projects.

Agile aims to keep everyone up to date about the state of play. It keeps everyone honest in the process. It makes you ask useful questions about the reality of your situation and forces you to uncover the true cost of what you are doing early enough for you to do some realistic cost benefit analysis. It often presents opportunities to uncover, encourage, increase and harness the creativity and skill of productive people.

Agile in context

What exactly is Agile?

This is the question to which just about everyone with a shtick to sell or a bone to pick is prepared to affix their sales pitches or prejudices. Yet it still seems to be a difficult one to get any consistent answer to. I understand the confusion, and sometimes outright hostility, from businesses and individuals who have only been exposed to this confusing babble and seemingly contradictory narrative.

What we are talking about here was not called Agile to start with. There were some approaches to developing software based on best practices that a community of interested people involved in high technology projects had begun to experiment with and share with each other. As this approach began to solve some long standing problems for these people, word spread. After a while it came to be called Agile.

Once there was an established brand, all sorts of methods and products began to label themselves "Agile" in order to join the party. Even methodologies against which Agile had been a reaction started hijacking the term Agile and redefining it to fit their product. As I write there are so many products and spin-offs that do not fit with the description "Agile" in any sense of the word that the term is becoming redundant.

Confused? Join the club. Nevertheless the thinking that launched Agile was sound. It describes the underlying philosophy of something that was a rational attempt to approach complex work in new technologies in a way that reflected the space and discipline that this work actually requires.

As we face challenges in business and technology the ideal needs to be reclaimed and restored to its former meaning – which is pretty much the meaning of the English word Agile:

> *To have a quick, resourceful and adaptable nature and the ability to move or change with quick and easy grace.*

Software development in a business context

Software development is difficult. There is no way around this fact. It is hard and it is getting harder as systems and technologies get more complex. Commercial software development usually takes place in the business environment it serves by keeping it in the commercial technology arms race. Business gives software development funding and a purpose.

Software development and business should be a natural fit and they would be if both software development and business were honest about their true nature and were to admit that they march to the beat of slightly different drums.

Software Development

Even in the most technology friendly of environments it takes a certain type of mind to develop software well. It demands a mixture of patience, honesty, logic, insight, perfectionism, arrogance and pig headedness. It demands fact based reasoning, an awareness of the consequences of mistakes and the ability to analyse cause and effect. Computers do not perceive, negotiate, gamble or guess. They are not HAL[6]. They simply do exactly what you tell them to do and they do not care what you meant to say or how you justify your logic. As systems get increasingly complex this propensity to do exactly what they are told makes them increasingly susceptible to woolly overblown requirements, guessing, gambling or half understood

---

6   The computer that went insane and with which the astronauts had to try to negotiate and humour in the film *2001 A Space Odyssey*

facts. Most commercial systems require teams of highly trained specialists working in a high state of collaboration. The fact that the computer is not analogous to a brain means that programming necessitates understanding how processors will carry out instructions over time, what the underlying logic is really going to do in different circumstances and how different systems and technologies will interact when the assumptions have been stripped down to the reality. It requires deep understanding, judgement, nerve, adaptability and experience.

Business

Many business people do not make the sort of hard headed, fact based decisions they would like us to believe they do. It's a sort of image they like to perpetuate in much the same way that professional gamblers like to maintain a poker face. Many of the most successful business people survive on a mixture of guts, decisiveness, bullshit and caffeine. Anyone who has ever had anything to do with the financial markets tells us that it is all about gambling and perception. Perception overrides fact.

Business, therefore, is a running gamble, what bookies call an accumulator[7]. If it were certain or if there were a foolproof formula for success, then everyone with half a brain would be a millionaire. As with gambling, business is about luck and the way the cards fall. The bank always wins. The tools of the trade have to be deep

---

7 An accumulator bet is one that links together two or more bets and is dependent on all bets winning. The output of one bet is the stake for the next. If one loses the whole thing collapses and there is no payout.

understanding, judgement, nerve, experience.

Change and dependency

The business world and the soft world are dealing with unprecedented rates of change. Information technology is busily following Moore's law[8] with accelerating levels of complexity, ability and expectation. Business is coming to terms with an increasingly reactive and fragile marketplace in which its bluff is regularly called. This is happening against a background of environmentally aware customers, energy concerns, social responsibility, political upheaval and economic chaos. New ways of working are required to bring IT and commerce into a mutually beneficial partnership. Agile is one way of seeking to create the essential bridge between the software engineer and the business person.

---

8   Moore's law roughly stated is that technology doubles in complexity every two years. Named after Gordon Moore who described it in 1965. He was talking about integrated circuits but it seems to apply to technology in general – memory, processing speed, pixels per inch are all improving exponentially.

Agile software engineering

The assertion I am making here will be controversial with many Agile providers and others. This assertion is that Agile[9] is best suited to developing software and particularly to developing software in a business environment. It was initiated and carried out by software developers who wanted their managers and business colleagues to:

1. Stop managing software projects as if they were in the manufacturing or building industry.
2. Recognise the nature of software development and respect its technical dependencies.
3. Plan for the time and resource it takes to do esoteric critical technical tasks properly.

---

9 Many, if not all, Agile principles are based on well known principles discovered to be true in many disciplines. As such, of course the principles are of generic value. However, what is discussed and sold as Agile is the application of these principles in Software Development. If you want to use these principles in other areas you need to go back to the underlying principles or there may be translation errors. Taking software development biased principles and practices and trying to apply them to other areas might sometimes work if the domains are sufficiently similar or there is a coincidental overlap. Most of the time it is like using an automatic translator to translate a biography, written in English then abridged and edited for a Russian market, into Russian and then trying to translate that book from Russian into French using another translation program. While the French might get some of the gist it will be fairly confused. You are always better to go back to the source, noting the reaction and insights from other domains. It is foolhardy to use a translation of a translation of a translation.

4. Budget for the technical overheads of working with badly designed and implemented legacy systems or systems that have simply become incompatible with new technology.

5. Acknowledge the value of excellence and dependability in business critical software. Balance that value against the perceived value of cost cutting essential skills and forcing unrealistic time-scales.

6. Be aware of the ongoing consequences of forcing developers to meet badly estimated time-scales with quick fixes and hastily engineered code bases.

7. Ask for metrics that are meaningful to the actual process of software engineering and recognise the waste of self perpetuating processes and management methodologies.

8. Express requirements as needs and desired outcomes rather than detailed instructions.

9. Approach project management as much more than an exercise in tracking budgets and enforcing plans. Think of it as exploring the best way to get the best result.

10. Recognise that business professionals and software professionals are colleagues not rivals. Dispense with the notion of the implied hierarchy of technology suppliers and business customers and combine business experience and technical experience on the same team.

The deadly embrace of intractability

Most of all Agile was embraced, practised and advanced by software developers who were passionate about their profession and who wanted to produce useful, maintainable and professional code that takes best advantage of the value of current technology. They wanted to be freed from the endless maintenance of badly implemented systems and the disrepute into which their profession was falling.

Badly designed code presents developers with an increasingly difficult to control medium. Not only is it difficult to control and work with, but it is very difficult to explain to a non technical person; especially those who dismiss software development as a commodity, service or a necessary evil. For the non technical person it often appears that the system simply works or does not work; and that it should be easy to make changes to it and extend it with seemingly reasonable new functionality requests. They are often surprised, alarmed and suspicious when new requirements break or destabilise the system. Managers can suspect developers of a kind of sabotage or incompetence. This can lead to distrust and the idea that more control is necessary. This control often takes the form of forcing developers into even tighter time-scales, increased auditing, tracking and micro-management. That in turn further damages the code base and deepens the suspicion and distrust of advice and estimates offered by the developer who is dealing with badly expressed requirements and people who do not respect or understand what they are asking the developer to do.

Developers can often dismiss this simply as bad management. They can lose respect for managers as a species. This encourages unprofessional behaviour as they are made to agree to design and structural compromises for short term gain on this project. They can even stop trying to design and develop it properly. The skills necessary to produce professional quality code can be lost through lack of practice and years of forced bad habit.

Badly executed code is not only unmaintainable but it breeds faults and bugs that cause the project to slip anyway. Agile was a way of saying to managers – "Look, you are going to keep slipping projects and producing more difficult to maintain systems by continuing with this command and control approach. Whether you believe us or not, things are going to get worse. Haven't you noticed how the difficulty factor is rising and how many projects need jury rigging at the end of the project to make them **almost** work? Regardless of the approach you take, you will be spending this time and money anyway – it is reality and you might as well get good systems for the investment. End to end the project will not cost you any more time or money if you let us do it properly. It just means being realistic about the technical realities and planning for them up front rather than paying the price later for not doing so. After a few cycles you will be amazed at the money you will be saving in maintenance costs and the value that technology will be delivering when we are freed of these legacy handcuffs that are foundering us all – let's call it **technical debt**. It is nobody's fault – we all allowed it to happen and we can fix it. We know code; you know what you need; let's talk."

Agile was an engineering discipline that sought to influence management style. It was not, and is not, a management style that influences engineering practices.

Software developers tend to be people who are naturally interested in following, understanding and using the advances of technology. What developers called Agile was defined by Kent Beck[10] as eXtreme Programming (XP). XP is full of immediate and useful techniques to deal with existing technical debt and to stop incurring more. It provides answers to the following:

- ☑ How to produce maintainable code with the highest business value.
- ☑ How to communicate estimates and issues to management and customers.
- ☑ How to organise technical teams.
- ☑ How to work with technical colleagues.
- ☑ How to push back against intractable process.
- ☑ How to educate yourself and your colleagues to deal with the constant advance of technology.
- ☑ How to deal with both reckless and lazy programmers on your project.
- ☑ How to deal with the technical realities of developing software in a business environment.

It was used with hefty doses of Pragmatic Programming[11] skills.

---

10 Kent's book "Extreme Programming Explained: Embrace Change" changed a lot of lives.

11 These are rather well described by Andrew Hunt and David Thomas in their book "The Pragmatic Programmer: From Journeyman to Master".

Agile becomes official

Agile Alliance

In a ski resort in Utah in 2001 representatives of what were then called "lightweight methodologies" got together to discuss the success of Extreme Programming and how they could build on it. They called themselves "The Agile Alliance" and they drafted the Agile Manifesto and the Agile principles.

My guess, particularly as an observer of what happened next, was that the wording of the principles was an attempt to keep everyone on the same page while soothing some large and disgruntled egos. They also had to hold on to the spirit of what was working. They managed to arrive at some positively stated outcomes that no one reasonable would take fright at. They took care not to hurt any feelings or create any conflict that might scupper the Agile Alliance at birth.

Stating things in the positive is generally a good idea, especially for people who really do adhere to the Agile manifesto to put individuals and interactions ahead of processes and tools. As Neville Chamberlain found out though, too much appeasement can cause more trouble and misunderstanding than straightforwardly calling a spade a spade and dealing with the consequences. This equivocating, placating and conciliating, while understandable in the early days, has continued and has allowed problems to surface and survive like a Trojan virus in Agile itself. In the Agile universe the language being used is becoming more and more divisive as various interests try to pretend that Agile is something other than it is. This has made it difficult to deal with genuine concerns and criticisms.

Answering the critics

Top 5 drawback of Agile according to its critics (and some of its apologists)

1. Agile does not have enough design and we might miss something.
2. Agile does not have enough documentation and we might lose something.
3. Agile does not scale up.
4. Agile was designed for software development.
5. Agile is a bottom up approach.

The first two are misinformed. The third is a semantic argument about what scaling up is. The last two are advantageous features.

1. Agile Design

When somebody is mounting an opera they need stage management, scenery, wardrobe, lighting, producers and a conductor. No one would be mad enough to suggest that just because the score is written down that you can pull in a pile of people off the street or half trained performers to perform it. Neither would they suggest that you try to convince the performers that practising is a waste of time.

Without the trained musicians in the orchestra and on stage, you can stage manage, direct, mount scenery and light it, push costumes around the stage and sell as many tickets as you like but you will not have a paying audience for long.

If a project were an opera production it would have a project manager taking the role of stage manager, hardware as scenery, project office as choreography, sales and marketing as box office, stakeholders as producers, and technical designer as conductor.

Of course there are librettists and composers in the form of the writers of the languages and the development tools.

All of this useless without the talent – the programmers are the musicians — and their playing and singing is what the punters are paying for. Undervalue, dismiss or sideline them at your peril.

Conducting design

A good conductor is one who understands the craft of making music and will understand musicians and singers. A good designer is one who understands code and coders. A good designer is one who respects the craft of programming, respects the structure and the integrity of the code and who will not force programmers to compromise it for a quick win.

Who the designer is depends on a number of factors. Among these are:

- The experience, confidence and skill level of the programmers.
- The size and scope of the project.
- The complexity of the system the new work is being integrated into.
- The stability of the technology being used.

The designer can be the programmer(s), the technical lead(s), in rare cases, the project manager and, if you are really lucky, you will have a person called a lead designer who understands the strategic and tactical direction of the system; who understands the architecture and is directing the evolution of the enterprise systems; and who is equally at home talking cost/benefit with stakeholders as with getting into the code with the developers.

A good designer in Agile will use Agile Modelling[12]. This is best implemented if the designer of the system gets together with the development team and sketches out the system design as it evolves. This is often carried out on a whiteboard that lives in the same location as the team.

In the best Agile teams I have worked with the design is an evolving team effort involving all of the above sharing responsibility for producing something they are proud of.

Design evolution

The idea that something as complex as a software system can be done without design is irritating. It breeds more stupidity and can only result in a state of stupor. What Agile tries to say about design is that it is better to evolve design than to predicate it based on the opinions of people who are not going to implement it and who do not understand the medium of code.

An Agile design is one that hangs the necessary pieces together loosely at the outset with recognition that even that might be wrong. It fills in the details as they become tangible. Dealing with the ideas, arguments and myths behind Agile design would take up this whole book (as would a discussion on "how do we know what we are getting for our money?") and then some. Let's just say here that Agile does involve design (and ensuring you get the best possible value for your money). Agile is a refinement of those things that are necessary and beneficial to software development. Most

---

12 Find details at www.agilemodeling.com

aspects of design are both necessary and beneficial. Design must be plugged into and aware of the medium it is designing for.

2. Agile documentation

I have never seen a programmer using the documentation to gain an understanding of the code. A programmer will always look first at the code itself because any documentation of the code, even it is miraculously up to date, will be a translation of the code and as with most translations it will be garbled and distorted in some way. In most cases it is utterly impossible to keep detailed documentation up to date with the code unless you have a totally restrictive change control process in place.

Programmers share pieces of code with each other when they want to share an idea. At most they will draw a few boxes on a whiteboard and scribble code underneath it. Well commented, articulate code is the only documentation that code needs; because the people who need to see documentation about code are programmers who understand the code better than they understand documentation. If they don't understand the code then the code needs to be refactored[13].

It is sometimes said that you need documentation so that new programmers can be brought up to speed quickly – go back to the paragraph beginning: "I have

---

13 A method of code evolution particularly effective in object orientated languages. It is a set of disciplined techniques that allow code to be restructured to facilitate efficiency, effectiveness, and **readability** of the code. It also improves the flexibility of the design. It should always reduce complexity and improve maintainability and extensibility of the code. It should never change the functional requirements of the code.

never seen a programmer using the documentation..."
please.

Systems documentation, user documentation, and
project documentation are different classes of
documentation. When Agile says it is document light it
does not really suggest not having these documents. The
proviso is that these documents limit themselves to
documenting what they say they are documenting.
Systems documentation should stay at the level of
systems components. User documentation should be
just that – how to use the system and where to get help.
Project documentation tracks budgets, time-scales,
delivery dates, milestones, constraints, roles,
responsibilities and risks – everything you might expect
or need to help you understand and track the project.

3. Scaling up Agile

This is a red herring often presented as if scaling
up Agile involved making it work in a waterfall
environment without making fundamental changes —
and of course it does not. Agile can work alongside
waterfall but in the end the projects most suited to Agile
should be allowed to move to it and the projects most
suited to waterfall should learn to cooperate with their
Agile colleagues. It will inevitably mean some deep
changes to any organisation with the vision to take this
path.

Scaling up Agile is often taken to mean making it
work in a command and control environment — and of
course it does not work well in a command and control
environment. Agile challenges the command and control
model as being a hindrance to getting anything
meaningful done.

Scaling up Agile often implies that size has to mean complexity. It is meant to represent the fact that using a hierarchical top down approach on something huge and complex delivers all sorts of headaches in terms or keeping track of, controlling and micromanaging people.

Agile challenges both of these ideas. If your Enterprise involves a supreme commanding Captain Kirk then scaling up Agile means that he has to spend more time listening to advice from engineering than issuing commands about the dilithium crystal.

In reality, scaling Agile to enterprise scale means dropping some of the ideas you have about what success looks like; or of success being the achievement of only one person's vision. Agile forces enterprises to face some truths about what the money is being spent on — it tends to flush out dead end projects and break down fiefdoms and mini empires.

If the truth were told, waterfall and command and control do not scale up and Agile is actually an intelligent answer to the bigger questions of how we deal with the requirements of managing the knowledge workers[14] necessary for business in the Information Age.

Scaling up Agile cannot be done by attempting to make it more complex. It can only be done by making it even more straightforward and letting go of some comfort blankets and the "Big Boss" image in order to become effective leaders.

---

14 The second book in T*he Trousers of Reality* series: *Managing Knowledge* deals with this head on.

4. Agile is for software development projects

Is this a problem? Not really. I think it is an advantage if you are developing software. It is only a drawback to two sets of people:

1. People who want to sell it as a panacea to all ills in all contexts without having to understand the target domain.

Of course you can use an Agile approach in different domains but you still have to have an understanding of that domain. In other words you have to have the equivalent of the engineering practices that spring from a deep understanding of the domain. Sorry folks – there is no tooth fairy, no free lunch and no silver bullet.

2. People who work in software development environments where the management are in denial and who are afraid to say it in case those managers will not engage.

Managers in companies dependent on IT need to face the fact that in the information age IT is software development and it is an integral part of their company. It is not a commodity that can be easily purchased off the shelf. At least when you do buy it off the shelf it is the same as buying a suit off the rack from a factory that makes one size fits all suits– you might be lucky but it is more likely that it will not fit properly. No product can be all things to all men, especially in IT, because of the transient nature of the technology and the changing nature of business, regulations and the marketplace. Tailoring and customising are always necessary.

5. Agile is a bottom up approach

This has the double meaning that Agile was invented by programmers and that good software design cannot be achieved by big design up front. Both of these statements are true.

Using the phrase "bottom up" when describing Agile as originating with professional programmers is a very telling phrase about how programmers are considered by the people who say it.

Using the phrase "bottom up" as a derogatory way to describe professional programmer driven software design is also very telling about how topsy turvy the attitude to IT has become.

Would you describe doctors diagnosing your illness and prescribing the correct medicine to be bottom up and you telling them you need steroids for an ingrowing toenail as top down?

If you mean that Agile originated with professional software developers keen to do their job, you would be correct.

If you mean that Agile maintains that good system designs must be based on properly crafted and structured code, you would be correct.

Appeasement

Agile has fallen victim to a perception of itself based on an apology to its critics rather than a clear statement of intent. This has led to some interesting myths and assumptions.

Agile Exposed

Assumptions that need addressing

The first is an assertion that there is a commodity called Agile and that any company can buy lots of it straight off the shelf.

There is no commodity called Agile. Agile is as manifestly difficult to certify, check, bottle or test as honesty. Agile is a made up term that attempts to bind a set of principles to a set of marketable brands. These brands have tried to create products from the wisdom of programmers and market them as magic ointment.

The second is that it is a management theory that allows you to gain control over programmers so that they will do more, do it faster and get it right with less resource and cost. The presupposition in this is that Agile does away with the need for knowledge of, or skill in, programming. This has led to a perennial clash of realities over off-shoring and Agile. Anyone who asks you about Agile and off-shoring in the same breath has just asked you how you can burn ice. Of course you can cover it in petrol or acquire some methane clathrate[15] and set fire to it but all you will achieve is lots of smoke and a damp carpet as the ice is transformed into a dirty puddle. Agile will not solve the problems introduced by

---

15 Methane Clathrate is ice in which methane has been trapped in water crystals and is known as "fire ice". It can burn but it releases methane and water. Huge methane releases can destabilise global temperatures and cause extinction of plant and animal life. Off-shoring implementation causes a similar catastrophic cycle. It disrupts the ecosystem of innovation. When R&D do not get meaningful feedback from production by seeing the process of production and the product they lose touch with reality and the foundations crumble.

off-shoring your most precious resource in the information age – skill and expertise in computer systems upon which your business depends for its life's blood.

If you are developing computer systems there is no substitute for skill and experience. There is no substitute for people who know their job and understand their customer. Agile depends on people who understand the realities of developing computer applications. It really does. It was developed to highlight this dependency; and you need to keep this in mind when deciding who to let introduce Agile (or any software development methodology) into your organisation.

Inertia and comforting lies

When people are used to doing things a certain way it is natural that there is inertia. Practice becomes habit and habits are difficult to break. Even if no one particularly likes the status quo they take the attitude of *"better the devil you know"*. Uncomfortable things can come to light when there is change. It often feels that organisations are stuck in a molasses of process and self deception that stops them from acting in their own long term interest.

Many organisations want the advantages of change but are fearful of actually changing anything. It is not surprising that snake oil salesmen thrive in this environment. They encourage the appearance of change but ultimately leave things as they are.

Too often the strategy seems to be to tell clients what they want to hear and spin out the contract as long as possible. This is understandable because telling clients the truth in the fog of disinformation around Agile and IT at the moment will get most honest consultants ejected from the premises. Clients favour someone who will weave the comforting story that nothing has to change and that you are doing everything just right: *"Here is a process for you to take in pill form. Just trust us and we will get out the Agile/Lean/SOA/Enterprise/Scrum stamp and make it all official."*

In many ways companies get the consultants they deserve.

Measuring Agility

I am frequently asked how to measure agility? Let me remind you of the Agile manifesto[16]:

"We are uncovering better ways of developing software by doing it and helping others do it. Through this work we have come to value:

- *Individuals and interactions over processes and tools*
- *Working software over comprehensive documentation*
- *Customer collaboration over contract negotiation*
- *Responding to change over following a plan*

That is, while there is value in the items on the right, we value the items on the left more."

It does not say "here are a set of licensed and certified things for you to emulate". It says "we are uncovering better ways of developing software by doing it".

Here are some suggestions of the things you can measure to see if you are focussed on helpful behaviours:

- Do your processes and tools facilitate or hinder your

---

16 Http://agilemanifesto.org

people working well together?
- Do you put more effort into the substantive content or the packaging of what you are doing?
- Do you grow your business by understanding your customers and delivering what they want or are you too busy checking the small print to make sure they can't get a refund?
- Is your organisation run by relaxed realists or uptight obsessive compulsives?

Management and Production

Business Overview of Projects

The Interface

Senior Management is exposed to the market, the economy, investors, regulation, competitors and a host of other pressures — including the way things are done — i.e. business traditions and habits. These traditions and habits are often wrapped up and delivered as processes and methodologies. These pressures and traditions bear down and force management to view their organisations through lenses of cost, time and progress against a plan. This leads to the organisation of work into packages commonly called projects.

Project Management is a highly skilled profession. It has its own battles with those who would reduce it to a compliance exercise in command and control. The interface between the essential management aspects and the production of aspects of companies can become very limited over time when the stereotype of managers and the managed become distorted to that of parents with unruly children. On IT projects this means that command and control methodologies often restrict communication to the language of compliance. Across this limited interface only conversations of time cost and progress can take place.

As this happens productivity is squeezed into a smaller and smaller space that often drastically compromises suitability of the end product.

Management has to deal with justifying the work, funding it, marketing and selling it while balancing it against a set of external pressures

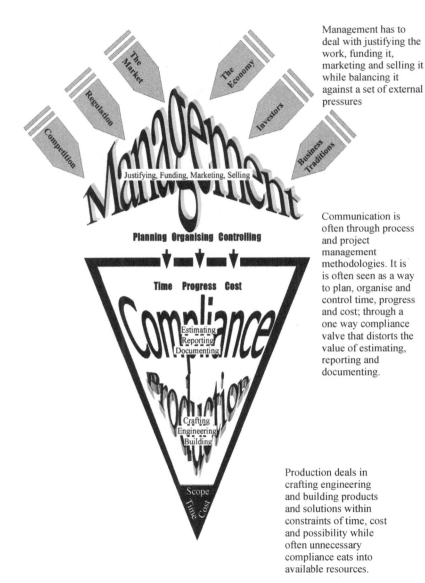

Communication is often through process and project management methodologies. It is is often seen as a way to plan, organise and control time, progress and cost; through a one way compliance valve that distorts the value of estimating, reporting and documenting.

Production deals in crafting engineering and building products and solutions within constraints of time, cost and possibility while often unnecessary compliance eats into available resources.

Cost – Time – Scope

The first two measures are easy enough to understand, quantify and control: *how long will it take and how much will it cost?* The third measure, scope, is a little more difficult to quantify, measure or control. Scope can be about many things — including functionality, completeness, quantity, quality and suitability (fitness for purpose). What the market can be persuaded to accept can sometimes be devoid of any of these as it relies on customer perception and ongoing shareholder profitability. These are transient and nebulous at best, especially to predict in advance.

Since time and cost are easy to report this leads many to rely on cost and time as the only reliable measure for how things are going and for steering their businesses.

Cost and time are easy things to plan, organise and control. Planning, organisation and control are the three pillars of project management according to just about everyone who hands out certification to project managers. Time, cost and scope are the sides of the iron triangle of project management. You can have only two of the three: good, fast or cheap.

1. FAST+CHEAP = BAD FIT

2. GOOD + FAST = EXPENSIVE

3. CHEAP+GOOD = SLOW

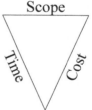

When you think you can control cost and time then the natural thing to do is to ignore 2 and 3 and redefine "Bad" in 1 to be scope. Therefore 1 becomes:

1. FAST+CHEAP = Whatever we can fit

The problem with this is apparent: the purpose of the project can often be at the mercy of arbitrary time-scales and cost cutting budgets.

Indeed there are certain Agile branded methodologies that wholeheartedly and mistakenly support this approach. Let's look a bit more at the project triangle before we move on to that.

The project triangle

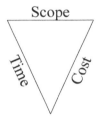

The project triangle, while satisfyingly simple, only tells part of the story. Anyone who has ever managed a project realises that there are many more factors at play. This being said, it is a good shorthand way to understand some of the decisions on a project and the thinking behind project management.

The project triangle tells us that if you make one of the sides rigid, then one or both of the other sides must move. This manifests mostly as projects that overrun on either time or cost or both time and cost. The reason for this is that many project plans cost and schedule everything into a plan that is so complex that actual progress or lack of it is not apparent, despite milestones, until late in the process. (See waterfall planning).

Time-boxing

Some vendors of Agile tools suggest that when project customers do not want to negotiate on requirements then quality suffers in a time and cost controlled environment.

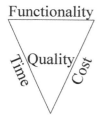

They suggest turning the triangle around so that time and cost are fixed and quality is preserved by constantly scoping, de-scoping and re-scoping.

This is called time-boxing and the hope is that you will have de-scoped, re-scoped and prioritised within small enough slices that the actual value of the functionality will have become apparent to either justify more investment or that the customer will be satisfied with the limited functionality delivered within the time-box.

Examining scope

On many projects, particularly software projects, people talk too easily about scoping things in and out as if it were only a matter of time and cost. There is a lot more to scope. My thesis is that time and cost are actually the support acts and that the main concern for project managers, stakeholders and everyone else concerned should be scope.

Scope has two meanings. The first is about observation as used in the words telescope, microscope etc. The second is about action. The first comes from the Greek *skopein*: to look. The second comes from the

Italian *scopo*: the purpose. We need to regard both meanings with equal interest.

Scope in a project is about intention, what we can see in order to plan; but more importantly scope is about maintainability and the deep structure of what we are doing – the scope is its ongoing purpose.

To really understand this in the context of software development we need to understand that software development is something new:

> ## *Software development is an ongoing conversation with technology!*

You might have noticed that when I talked about the project triangle in a time-boxing context, the third leg became functionality not scope. This is because Rapid Application Development (RAD)[17], which is sometimes confused with Agile and upon which some Agile methodologies are clearly based, separates quality out from scope. Agile approaches based on RAD also try to separate quality from scope, but this would seem to me to be a mistake.

If we accept the basic principles upon which Agile is based then scope must include quality. Quality in software development is not just about the quality of the product from the user perspective; it is also about the structure of the product from a technical perspective. It is the measure of how brittle or adaptable the code is and how well it will deal with the advance of business and technology.

---

17 See "RAD — Rapid Application Development" on page 122 for an explanation of RAD

You can scope and de-scope individual functionality but you cannot scope or de-scope scope. You can only increase and diminish the scope of the project as a whole.

The intrinsic scope of every software project is not only to exploit current levels of technology; the intrinsic scope of a software project is to keep the lines of communication clear for future conversations.

This is a critical distinction in identifying and exposing Agile hype. It is also essential in understanding what Agile is trying to address and why it works when it works.

There is something of a sleight of hand going on when the project triangle is talked about by certain Agile methodologies and trainers. If scope is confused with functionality then this allows quality to be presented as a fourth side in the triangle. While it might initially cause some people to accept an oversimplified version of Agile that promises to deliver things faster and cheaper, there is no such thing as a free lunch. As I have said, in this universe the law of conservation of energy applies and you cannot get something for nothing.

If you are presented with the following as the realities of a project triangle, what has happened is that scope has already been de-constructed, rearranged and selectively presented as functionality.

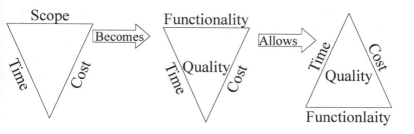

Scope is an entity composed of quality and functionality. The label scope has been hijacked in a successful attempt to distract everyone from what actually happens on projects and substitute semantic arguments for real decisions. Scope has been sundered in the imagination of erstwhile methodologists and now just means functionality. This process allows quality to be considered some sort of optional extra that can be manipulated. It is balderdash that allows hype and chicanery.

I propose "usefulness" as a better way to think of the basic unit of scope.

Functionality that is not useful is not worthwhile no matter how cheap it is, no matter how quickly you can have and no matter how much of it there is.

Reading this you might think that it is a self evident truth. You would be surprised how many pragmatists and hard nosed negotiators miss it. You would be amazed at how many times we are convinced of the opposite at the hands of the unscrupulous. How many times in life do all of us accept cheap and fast instead of insisting on what we want and know we need? How often does the bargain end up costing more, wasting our time and creating an obstacle to us getting what we need?

Quality that is not useful is not worthwhile no matter how cheap it is and no matter how quickly you can have it.

This is a consequence of separating functionality and quality within scope. Quality, as in persistent usefulness, is a consequence of what you decide to do and how you do it. It is the arbiter of scope.

What about time?

We could also sunder time in many ways to create a fourth side of the triangle. Most commonly on projects it is split into man hours and elapsed time. This creates the following semantic slight of hand in estimating how long a thing will take by confusing efficiency with effectiveness:

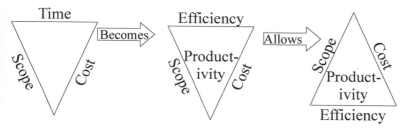

Time is a consequence of entropy and you cannot change its nature. No matter whether you use backlogs, plans, a carrot or a whip, things take as long as they take. Even if you would like to deal in man hours you pay for elapsed time. The real world deals in elapsed time which rolls merrily along while we are busily being human.

Productivity that is not useful is not worthwhile no matter how cheap it is and regardless of its quality.

There is a consequence to separating efficient time from elapsed time. Productivity, as in persistent usefulness, is a consequence of what you decide to do and how you do it. It is the arbiter of how long it will take you to do something, not the other way round.

What about cost?

We could sunder cost in many ways to create a fourth side of the triangle. Most commonly we split cost into direct investment and running costs. This allows the following slight of hand in calculating return on investment or value for money.

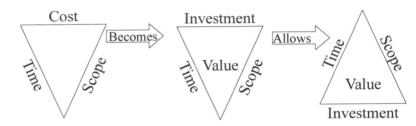

There is much to say about the finances of projects, budgets and the effects of things like Agile on project accounting, but it all boils down to this:

You might scrap this project or that one because the return on the investment does not seem worthwhile. In the background, especially in large companies, the costs do not suspend themselves. If you are not counting the whole cost to your capital investments, staff salaries, future maintenance costs and lost opportunities through de-motivation, you have nothing to say about value.

Value that is not useful is not worthwhile regardless of the quality and no matter how quickly you can have it.

This is a consequence of separating tangible costs from intangible ones. Value, as in persistent usefulness, is a consequence of what you decide to do and how you do it. It is the arbiter of cost not the other way round.

More than the sum of its parts

Usefulness>quality+productivity+value

Quality, productivity and value are all desirable outcomes from any endeavour defined by time, cost and scope but only if they are tempered by usefulness. When Agile or anything else tries to tell you that usefulness is negotiable then someone is fooling someone and there is some kind of dissimulation going on. In other words hype is a distortion of the truth.

Anything which takes the easy path of strengthening misguided prejudice and reinforcing the problem rather than clearing the way for a solution is dishonest. Usefulness comes about through understanding what is useful — and achieving this is a matter of open communication. This is how you effect quality: remove obstacles to communicating and understanding: especially if they are eating the resources you should be using to get things done. Go from this:

To this:

Management still has to deal with external pressures but now it has more accurate and up to date information based on what is really going on in the organisation.

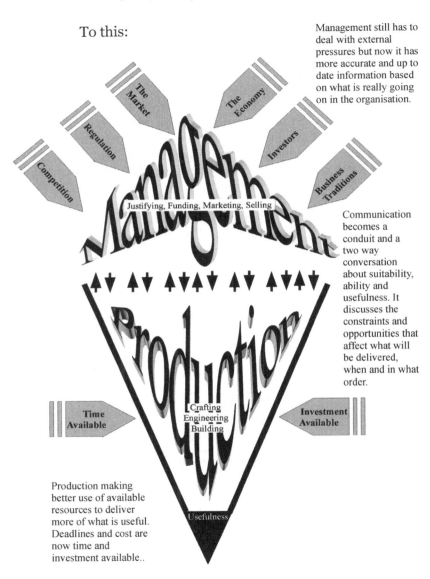

Justifying, Funding, Marketing, Selling

Communication becomes a conduit and a two way conversation about suitability, ability and usefulness. It discusses the constraints and opportunities that affect what will be delivered, when and in what order.

Crafting
Engineering
Building

Production making better use of available resources to deliver more of what is useful. Deadlines and cost are now time and investment available..

Conclusion

So what is Agile?

Agile is a way of recognising and respecting complexity. It is a way to deal with complexity. It is an acceptance that you cannot fight fire with fire: you cannot deal with complexity by adding more complexity. You fight a fire with its opposite – water. You manage complexity with simplicity. Agile is applied simplicity. This simplicity reaches for the elegance of nature.

"Human subtlety...will never devise an invention more beautiful, more simple or more direct than does nature, because in her inventions nothing is lacking, and nothing is superfluous."
Leonardo Da Vinci
(1452-1519)
Genius

Agile is evolution harnessed. It uses the laws of natural selection, which is not the survival of the fittest but the self organisation of resources into the best fit for the environment. Agile is a way to make your bad programmers good, your good programmers excellent and your excellent programmers stay.

It is a way of uncovering the ability in your organisation to encourage balance between the rights of the customer, the risks of the entrepreneur and the skills of the programmer. Agile is a way of examining and eliminating prejudices and limiting beliefs that can cripple productivity and effectiveness. It is a way for business to engage with the demands and rewards of the information age.

If you remember at least one thing from this book let it be:

> ### *Software development is an ongoing conversation with technology!*

Software developers represent your business in that conversation. They are explorers, negotiators, navigators, interpreters, protectors, translators, guides and mapmakers. Treat them as trusted and talented allies because you really need their help to take part in that conversation.

Part Two – Agile Analysed

Guide to Agile Methods

The Agile umbrella

Reviews

These are my opinions, having come into contact and having used these tools. My opinions are biased, personal and selective. Just like any reviews they are based on my experiences and judgement.

Some of the following methods claim to be Agile as in a noun rather than an adjective. If you have an Agile outcome in mind and you understand what you are aiming for, then some of them have practices and techniques that can lead to you doing things agilely (the adverb). Simply following any of them as a process will not deliver the real benefits of Agile.

There is no such thing as a free lunch or a perpetual motion machine. The laws of conservation of energy apply in our universe and that includes software development and business. You cannot get more for less. Creating value from nothing is a matter of selling perceptions and was dealt with in the old story "The Emperor's New Clothes".

Agile methodology is an oxymoron

Agile is not a methodology so much as an attitude and an approach. It borders on being a philosophy about how to work with technology, knowledge workers and progress.

This leads to some confusion as to what to label the tools, practices and patterns of behaviour that emerge from this approach. These are recorded and passed on so that not everyone has to reinvent the wheel and can press forward with the underlying business of managing change.

Some people have suggested that "Agile methods" is a functional description since they are a set of tools that work well together but are not confined to a proscriptive process. When Agile methods forget this and present themselves as a process or methodology there can be unwelcome outcomes since whatever you label this behaviour, following a process or methodology is not as effective as thinking.

When you think about methods for developing software in an Agile environment some of the things you really need to consider are:

- The importance of understanding the domain.
- The importance of properly structured code.
- The importance of communications.
- The importance of non-functional requirements as well as the functional ones.
- The importance of non tangible as well as tangible benefits.
- The importance of a technical perspective.
- The importance of the business environment.
- The importance of sustainability and learning.

User stories

What are they?

User stories[18] are a way to express requirements in the language of customers as requests with outcome-focussed promises of work.

They are generally presented in the following format on a single index card with the acceptance criteria on the reverse:

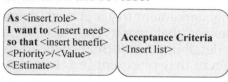

Each story has an estimate and a value. Acceptance criteria must be testable in a way that the developer, customer and user will all know when the requirement has been delivered.

Unique features

User stories are crafted to be:
- Independent
- Negotiable
- Valuable[19]
- Estimable
- Small
- Testable

By a strange coincidence these make up the handy acronym INVEST.

---

18 Mike Cohn's book "User Stores Applied for Agile Software Development"– is a great source of information on how to use these effectively.

19 Can also be called vertical - no horizontal dependencies i.e. independent.

Are they useful?

They can be used to facilitate the scheduling of work into iterations and to highlight and manage dependencies between pieces of work. They can be used to organise requirements into deliverable units of functionality. They allow work to be quantified and prioritised and are at their best when they are estimated relative to each other so that expectations about progress and delivery dates can be managed.

They are best described as a place-holder for work to be done and a mutual agreement to get enough detail to understand and deliver that work. They are often accompanied by more detail in other formats depending on the type of requirement they represent (e.g. technical requirements may carry information about data sources and types in associated documents or databases; user interface requirements may carry results of market research or focus groups that will drive the ergonomics and screen design etc).

Under what conditions?

They work well as part of an overall Agile approach. They are not documentation – they are metaphors that represent delivered functionality. As such they allow work to be packaged, prioritised and scoped in a very flexible way.

When they are treated as a flexible technique that predicates a certain level of skill and experience they work really well.

When the implementation realities are respected and understood they are effective. Whoever is using them needs to understand and be able to quantify the consequences of delivering functionality out of natural sequence and be qualified to decide whether the cost and consequences are justified.

When it is understood that they are not documentation and that new user stories can replace old ones, they can be used efficiently.

User stories sit as a representation of things to be done that can be scoped in and out of iterations. There are a number of techniques to do this and to decide how many and how big they should be depending on your approach to Agile.

Contra indications

User stories are the craft knife of Agile – the tool of a surgeon or a murderer. They can be the either the critical ingredient or the poison that kills the project depending on who is using them and how. They can sometimes become part of the problem. Here are some examples:

- If they are treated as a shorthand way to capture requirements, they can be misleading. They are not requirements – they represent requirements. They represent the investigation, collaboration and evolution that need to happen. A good user story never claims to have captured the requirement – just the outcome desired with its relative cost and value as known at present.
- If they are prioritised and scoped without respect for technical or non-functional requirements, they can be used as a micromanagement tool or to force work that will cause damage to the code base.
- If existing waterfall requirements are simply transcribed into the user story format, there is no gain.

- If they are prioritised and managed as mini waterfall requirements without the collaborative, investigative and evolutionary ingredients, unnecessary things will be done, other things will be missed and bad design decisions will be made which will compromise the integrity of the code and the possibility of delivery.
- If they are presented as a formula, process or a set of unbending rules about presentation and prioritisation they will cause miscommunication and confusion.
- If they give the impression that things can be done in any whimsical order they can cause problems. Sometimes there are unavoidable technical or real world dependencies. Although it may be theoretically possible to do things out of order, the design and financial consequences can be catastrophic for a project or a system.

Agile stars ✪ ✪ ✪ ✪

I give user stories 4 out of 5. They provide an essential communication tool and can create real space for discussion and learning in Agile planning. Mike Cohn has done a remarkable job of taking a concept from early Agile and adapting it in new and exciting ways that clearly explain what Agile is all about.

I did not give then that final star because user stories are often used as a means to ignore and undermine implementation issues. They can become a process that causes customers, Agile coaches and project managers to assert that the customer is always right. The customer is not always right and is frequently wrong and needs to listen to people who understand the consequences and cost of decisions that force technical direction.

Scrum

What is it?

It is a lightweight planning, prioritisation and progress tracking process, packaged and marketed as a methodology.

Agile Features

In common with other Agile approaches it has these features:

- Iterations headed and tailed with planning meetings and retrospectives.
- Learning through feedback.
- Framework for User Stories.
- Products and product owners rather than projects and project managers.
- Focus on value to the customer.
- Prioritisation.

Unique features

- Hierarchical reporting – scrums (daily team stand-ups) and scrums of scrums (daily stand-ups of team leaders) etc.
- Restriction of all work to a plan called a prioritised backlog often made up of user stories.

Is it useful?

It can be quite a useful facilitation tool in the early days of Agile introduction as a way to warm traditional managers to the idea of involving customers and technical people in estimating and planning discussions whilst maintaining a "command and control light" approach. It can open the door to more useful Agile methods.

Under what circumstances?

When it is implemented by a person with a full 360 degree understanding of the domain it can add value. In a Software Development environment that would be someone who understands the realities of software engineering and who also understands or works closely with someone who understands the commercial realities of the business, the customers and the market.

Contra indications

Many of the problems and contra indications for Scrum arise not from inherit problems with Scrum as a project facilitation tool but with how it is marketed and sold. This drives:
- How it is implemented.
- Who implements it.
- Where it is implemented.
- What it is implemented as.
- What level it is implemented at.
- Expectations about what it can achieve.

Specifically:
- **Rigidity.** Scrum uses a rigid, if somewhat simplistic, process with a rules based approach. This means that it can fall between the two stools of command and control and Agile while satisfying neither.

- **Management Tool**. Scrum can easily implement Agile at the wrong level and teach the wrong lessons. It is sold and marketed as a project management methodology and a management tool. It can easily become a vehicle for project micromanagement and command and control behaviour.
- **In the wrong hands:** When managers are unwilling to let go of the reins Scrum offers them a way to rigidly insist on rules:
  - Daily scrums driven from a purely progress-against-the-plan mentality can become witch hunts and homework-excuse sessions.
  - While prioritisation is a good thing people are not robots and should not be treated as such. As pointed out throughout this book software development is a difficult, exploratory and creative endeavour that cannot be forced. Programmers often find that they need to concentrate on something not on the critical path but related to the task in hand for a while, in order to free their mental impasse and search for inspiration. By the time this work gets put on the backlog and rescheduled, as scrum suggests, many opportunities can be missed.
- **Jumps the shark and nukes the fridge**[20]. Scrum is a facilitation process with pretensions of being a methodology. It tries to be all things to all men and frequently punches above its weight. When it is treated as a set of rules for implementing Agile it is not detailed enough and fails to address many of the issues that Agile seeks address.

---

20 To abandon the ethos and inner logic that made something useful or popular in the first place. Something whose grasp now exceeds its reach.

- **The issue of technical debt** – Scrum exacerbates this issue because it focuses on priority and speed at the expense of the engineering practises that produce properly structured code.
- **Communication issues** — Scrum often limits the discussion to the same limited views of project management that have caused problems for waterfall i.e. time, cost and progress against a plan – now called a prioritised backlog.
- **Certification issues** – Scrum's main product is a 2 day scrum master certification training course that exploits the problem of certification replacing actual ability or knowledge. Attendance of this course guarantees certification irrespective of any prior lack of experience or missing knowledge about software development or Agile. These "Masters" of scrum can sometimes take over the running of software projects on the basis of this training.

• **Window dressing.** The benefits of Agile – responsiveness to new requirements, low maintenance costs and rapid reaction to business opportunities – are enabled by a strong, flexible and well structured code base. Everything else is window dressing. Scrum focuses on the window dressing of Agile ceremony while claiming the benefits of building the shop.

Agile stars ✬

My score is 1 out of 5. I would give this a higher mark but for the fact that it is primarily a business concerned with making money for Scrum organisations. Check out the pricing and conditions on the scrum alliance web-site for the costs involved in scrum master certification. The current conditions to become a certified trainer that hands out scrum certifications are allegiance to Scrum, a pay-per-attendant licence fee when you train and a fee of $7,500 per year to hold the Certified Scrum Trainer qualification.

There is a concern that Scrum is so focussed on fast delivery through prioritisation on business value that it ignores the diminishing quality of the code base. In my experience Scrum coasts along on a wave of deliberately created Hawthorne effect[21] and the fuel still in the tank from the efforts of past developers. Without paying close attention to the branch on which you are standing, in this case the code and the systems architecture, sooner or later things are going to drop out from under you.

My final analysis of Scrum is that its days are numbered. You can only sell buns and sauce for so long before someone notices that there is no hot-dog.

---

21 The Hawthorn Effect: People often perform better when they know they are the subjects of an experiment. Based on the work of Mayo and Roethlisberger at the Hawthorne factory between 1927 and 1932 it is still the subject of evaluation and interpretation.

DSDM

What is it?

Dynamic Systems Development Methodology (DSDM)[22]. This is possibly the oldest of the methodologies currently sheltering under the Agile umbrella. It focuses on projects with tight time-scales and budgets. Its latest incarnation is DSDM Atern (named after the Arctic Tern which is apparently a collaborative bird).

Unique features

- **Feasibility phase:** Unlike the other Agile methodologies it has a feasibility phase in which you decide if the project is suitable for DSDM.
- *MoSCoW:* Its most valuable contribution in my opinion is the idea of *MoSCoW*'ing requirements i.e. applying categorisation under the following headings for further prioritisation.
  - **M**ust have (essential features)
  - **S**hould have (valuable but not essential features)
  - **C**ould have (Nice to have but not really valuable or essential)
  - **W**ould/won't have unless we really have nothing better to do.
- **Time-boxes**: DSDM also brings us the idea of time-boxing. Time-boxing comes from Rapid Application Development (RAD) and rests on the project triangle. The idea is to deliver the best complete functionality you can within the time allowed. In RAD it is

---

22 Find detail at www.dsdm.org

supposed to curtail the perfectionist tendencies of programmers and deliver systems that are just good enough as fast as possible.

Is it useful?

It occupies the same space as SCRUM although I find it to be more honest about what it is. The training on offer seems to be varied with more depth. It acknowledges and tries to address traditional issues of project management.

Under what circumstances?

DSDM has different project phases
- Feasibility and business study
- Build functional prototypes
- Design and build
- Implement/deploy/maintain

Each phase iterates until it finishes. This hybrid approach makes it quite a useful bridge methodology for waterfall dependent companies thinking about Agile but not ready to commit.

Contra indications

It claims to be perfectly compatible with both PRINCE2 and Extreme programming. On examination the compatibility is more with PRINCE2. It can fall into the trap of not giving enough importance to the structure of the code – particularly with its use of prototypes and its phased approach separating design from implementation.

Agile Stars ✩✩

I give it 2 out of five Agile stars because MoSCoW, Time-boxing and the feasibility study can be useful on Agile projects. It offers an easy transition from waterfall. It is more Rapid Application Development (RAD)[23] than Agile though. Although it has Agile aspects it is getting increasingly complex and less Agile every time I look at it.

All this being said I must say that DSDM is honest about what it is, how it works and it even tells you that it is not suitable for every project. As a project management methodology I rate it quite highly on those projects for which it is suitable. It is a vast improvement on many waterfall methodologies. My opinion is that it does a valuable job humanising PRINCE2. I also take it more seriously because it is trying to evolve, adapt and respond to its critics and does not rely on an oversimplified and easy to sell formula.

---

23 See "RAD — Rapid Application Development" on page 122

PRINCE2

What is it?

PRojects IN Controlled Environments. This often tries to smuggle itself under the Agile umbrella. It is a heavyweight pre-Agile process based methodology concerned with control and management aspects of projects. It sees its role as planning, delegating, monitoring and controlling. It is clearly a waterfall methodology. It is keen on documentation and rules that force compliance with the constraints it introduces. Whatever is not expressly authorised is strictly forbidden. It supports top down hierarchies and tools to control people. It treats creative people as a risk to be contained and this especially includes programmers.

The original PRINCE was launched in 1989 to replace PROMPT (Project Organisation Management Planning Technique) to carry out government projects in the UK. It suits control freaks and organisations who totally distrust their staff and is a clear indication that they think they have employed morons. It has certifications and trainings to delight even the most hide-bound bureaucrat. It is very effective at doing what it says on the tin – controlling and restricting risk — if you define creativity or inspiration as risk.

Quite a few PRINCE2 practitioners claim that it works well with DSDM Atern. I can't help but think of image of little DSDM holding beefy PRINCE2 's coat while it batters some project into submission[24].

---

24 I know this is probably not entirely fair but it is an amusing image.

Unique features

Quite frankly it boggles the imagination how this can even try to label itself as Agile. It is like a 22 stone weight lifter claiming to be a ballerina by wearing a tutu.

Is it useful?

Yes – to implement waterfall project management or as a tool-kit you can cannibalise.

Under what circumstances?

Although waterfall command and control methodologies are contraindicated on Agile projects, waterfall has tools that can be used on any project. Establishing terms of reference, setting out the business case and critical path analysis to name a few. You could regard PRINCE2 as one tool-kit of things that have been developed to deal with very specific circumstances. The danger in that is that if you have an expensive hammer then everything you have to do starts looking like a nail.

Contra indications

Agile projects.
PRINCE tends smother Agile software development practices and makes them next to impossible. The process and the attendant politics in PRINCE prevents the realisation of the real benefits of Agile which depend on light and flexible process.

Agile stars

0/5: I give it 0 out of 5 stars as an Agile methodology.

If this book were about waterfall project management methodologies I would give PRINCE a much higher mark as a waterfall project management methodology, because that is what it is.

Lean

What is it?

Lean[25] is based on the worthy ideas of W Edwards Demming as expanded on and used in the Toyota factories in Japan.

Unique features

- The seven wastes (purists use the Japanese word muda) defined by Taiichi Ohno of Toyota

    ○ Rework (defects)
    ○ Overproduction
    ○ Transport
    ○ Waiting
    ○ Inventory
    ○ Motion
    ○ Over-processing

Is it useful?

It can be a very useful thought exercise to consider how waste can hide in plain view and to consider that overproduction is actually a waste. I really value the lessons I learned from the Theory of Constraints to which Lean is related so I continue to have a soft spot for Lean. Taken as a tool-bag of techniques that can be applied to different problems that can arise, it has a great deal of value. As a methodology for software development – I am not so sure.

---

25 Find details at www.lean.org

Unfortunately it is in danger of converting itself into a 21st century version of scientific management with its unhealthy obsession with identifying everything without a cash value as waste. This opens the door to identifying everything not directly profitable (such as taking time out to think) as waste. It can look suspiciously like time and motion[26] when one of its main tenets of faith is to cut costs at all cost.

Under what circumstances?

As with Scrum, it is a totalitarian regime. When I talk to some Lean purists I can't help picturing the Borg[27]; although I think they are aiming at being the

---

26 Imagine someone standing over you with a stopwatch while you work, timing everything you do and looking for ways to get more work out of you. Time and motion is a tool of Taylorism and Scientific Management (discussed in Volume One of the Trousers of Reality). It seeks to constantly increase the pace of productivity of human labour. It measures the time to do tasks and arrives at standard timings based on the fastest workers. It decides which tasks are increasing productivity based solely on output. In its heyday people were even timed during toilet breaks and toilet doors were removed so that they would not take more than their allotted time. It treats people as automata and work units and has generated huge rifts between workforces and their management. It is a manufacturing technique still championed by some as a way to increase productivity and eliminate waste; but it has no place at all in knowledge work. It is counter productive to dehumanise people in any endeavour. This sort of efficiency leads only to very short term productivity if at all.

27 The Borg: Star Trek baddies obsessed with eliminating biological weaknesses to achieve an unemotional and mechanical perfection by assimilating or eliminating anyone they consider to be a wasting resources.

Vulcans[28]. Early in my career I had to deal with a lot of WISSCS managers (Why isn't somebody somewhere coding something) who would prefer their employees to be visibly busy and considered all forms of thought, investigation, training and talk to be a waste of good typing time. They also measured productivity by lines of code.

The bottom line is that Demming is essential reading for anyone involved in business and in the business of managing people. Lean's manufacturing emphasis and manufacturing metaphor causes it to treat software development as the production of software systems as quickly and as cheaply as possible. This ignores any sort of job satisfaction, creativity and longer term benefits associated with them. Lean takes a step in the wrong direction as the steps of manufacturing lead software development back to waterfall and component optimisation. Ironically, Lean pays a lot of lip service to systems thinking but immediately limits the system to Lean: cutting cost through eliminating waste which opens the door to time and motion style processes depending on who is deciding what is waste.

Contra indications

Lean has some great ideas and some interesting things to bring to the table — but honestly, while Japanese culture excels in many ways, have a look at the levels of stress and suicide in their efficient society

---

28 The Vulcans: Star Trek goodies who eliminated emotion because they see it as wasteful and confusing. In their distant history it was linked with barbarism. They are portrayed as being motivated by pure logic and reason. One might say that getting rid of emotion altogether might have been a bit of an over reaction – akin to throwing out the baby with the bathwater – exactly my concern for Lean.

before buying wholesale into the Lean vision of Japanese efficiency.

Agile stars ⋆⋆

I give it 2 out of 5 because Demming was a true visionary and his ideas about dealing with motivation and management in business are still relevant and valuable.

My analysis of Lean is that it is very real danger of becoming Scrum 2.0 in attitude and the zombie of scientific management in deed. It is based on very sound manufacturing insights that could help uncover helpful principles if it can come down from the mountain and stop preaching, if it can realise that software development is not manufacturing and if it can acknowledge and that bottom line profitability is not the only reason or even the best reason to do things or the only measure to prioritise them by.

Kanban

What is it?

Kanban[29] is the Japanese word for the token used in stock control to tell you that if you order now you will have enough stock to last you until the new delivery arrives. It is a part of Just In Time (JIT) manufacturing. Kanban is also a Lean, post-Agile technique that uses post-its on a board to indicate what is in play, waiting to come into play and delivered.

Unique features

- **Kanban board** – Work, represented by post-its, move through the following columns:
  - In progress
  - In test
  - Ready for release
  - Released
- **WIP (work in progress) limi**t – this measures the limit of work that can enter any column and is a way of identifying bottlenecks in the process.

Is it useful?

By all means explore Kanban as an advanced technique when you really understand what Agile is all about but be aware that it is a manufacturing concept.

Under what circumstances?

It might be okay with top of the range programmers. It assumes stable technology and a high

29 Find details at www.kanban101.com/

level of skill in what you are doing. I see Kanban working only with some other Agile and project management safeguards.

Contra Indications

Some Kanbanners I know eschew estimation and planning by taking the view that things take as long as they take and it's nobody else's business. Business people who are managing budgets need to have some idea of how long something is going to take and therefore estimates are at the very least an essential courtesy.

Agile stars ✬✬

I give it 2 out of 5 because I know people who make it work but with the caveat that it is a tool not a methodology or even a method.

Extreme Programming (XP)

What is it?

XP[30] is a fully functional set of software engineering and management guidance tools based on recognised best practices. It focuses on two things:
- The quality, extensibility and maintainability of the code base
- Opening the bandwidth of communications and understanding between business and technical people.

Unique Features

The "Extreme" in the name comes from the underlying technique of turning the dial up to maximum on all best practices. The extreme allows you to get maximum benefit from good techniques.

- **Test first programming**[31] — testing is good so do it all the time – the extreme measure is to write tests before the code as a guide to code design and structural integrity.

- **Continuous integration** — integrating code as early as possible is a good practice so that possible conflicts and requirements are understood and resolved– the extreme measure is to do it all the time so there is no build up of technical debt that might compromise delivery.

- **Pair programming** – code reviews are essential to check for cognitive dissonance or mistakes. Sharing

---

30 Find details at *www.**extremeprogramming**.org/*
31 See "A short note on TFP and TDD" on page 107 for a more detailed explanation.

standards and code ownership is a necessary practice. The extreme measure is that all code is written by pairs. Programmers program with a different team member every day and circulate through the whole team so that everyone understands the whole code base.

- Responsibility and code comprehension is shared and best practices percolate.
- While at first it may seem counter intuitive to double up resources on tasks, code produced like this is less prone to bugs, easier to read, better structured and usually has a high coverage of unit tests.
- If we measure end to end delivery of functionality and ease of maintenance rather than individual tasks, not only is there an increase in overall productivity but there is a significant cost saving.
- Code tends to be leaner and fitter for purpose, there is less of it to maintain and developers rarely get the programming equivalent of writer's block.
- Everyone in the team has the expertise to work on any part of the system so that holidays, sickness and staff turnover is easier to manage.

- **Small iterative deliveries** — Delivering functionality is good — the extreme measure is to deliver a working system in the form of the smallest complete units of useful functionality possible at the end of every cycle.

- **Refactoring** – Maintainable, extensible and easily understandable code is good. Well designed and well structured code is invaluable – the extreme measure is to constantly tend the underlying code base and improve the structure and design of even legacy code.

Refactoring[32] tends to implement well understood structural patterns to make the underlying code cleaner and more maintainable while preserving the functionality. Depends heavily on a complete coverage of unit and integration tests to protect functionality.

- **Daily stand-up** – communication, transparency and the reporting of important information as early as possible to people who need it to make decisions is good. The extreme measure is that the people doing the work report on their progress every day to each other and to anyone with an interest in what they are doing. They keep it short and talk only about what they have done since the last daily stand-up and what they plan to do before the next one. They also alert everyone to any issues, puzzles, delays or problems that are inhibiting progress or threatening to.
- **Planning game** – accurate and realistic planning is necessary. The extreme measure is to do it all the time. Release and iteration planning is done with customers and technical people in a stress free environment where everyone involved with the project is free to speak their mind.
  - The key to this is that the people who will be coding make the estimates and the people paying for it specify the value and priority of requirements. Business people make business decisions and technical people make technical decisions – all parties must acknowledge that these have internal dependencies.
  - *Technical* requirements and *non-functional* requirements which do not appear to have much value to the purse holder can cause novices to fret a

---

32 Martin Fowler's book "Refactoring: Improving the Design of Existing Code" is the bible for this.

bit. This is easily resolved if you realise that these things belong in the technical decisions and estimates. Business people must trust the technical people to make technical decisions that will support their business value decisions.

- Technical people to provide the simplest solution that will meet the requirements. This must be as simple as possible and not be forced to be any more simple. This is a technical call.

- **Retrospectives and velocity** — understanding the impact of what we are doing and our real capability is good – the extreme measure is to hold retrospectives to examine what worked, how it worked and how we could do it better. XP also measures progress in a meaningful way to provide guidance for people who have to balance budgets and manage resources and milestones. This is called team velocity.

- **On-site customer** — understanding the customer, communicating progress, respecting their wishes and communicating consequences to them is good – the extreme measure is to collaborate and communicate with the customer or the customer representative as a part of the team.

Is it useful?

It is honest about its relationship with software development. It grasps the nettle and immediately starts offering solid advice about how to craft great code. It spans project management and programming. It welcomes suggestions about both as long as the fundamental realities of software engineering are respected: software development and responding to change relies on a code base that is well structured, well tested and maintainable. It does not pretend to be a project management methodology but it can be used to guide project management toward good decisions in a software development environment.

Under what circumstances?

In software development environments where perfect can be approached as a verb not an adjective. Where other methodologies only offer ways to contain and control change XP is explicitly about understanding and exploiting the ability and necessity of software to change with technology, business, progress and entropy.

Contra indications

It is sometimes pointed out that XP has internal dependencies and that you need to do it all to get any benefit. This is quite true. However, paradoxically, XP is not proscriptive. It is based on the realities of software development and it is focussed on the outcomes. Each practice has an outcome but those outcomes, on any sort of inspection, are outcomes that are necessary for the development of successful software systems. All of these are related to the end product:

- Systems and the code of which they are comprised:
  - Maintainable code.
  - Flexible extensible code.
  - Working code.
  - Bug free code.
  - People capable of understanding and working with code.
  - Code that delivers critical, valuable and timely functionality.
  - Code that can be integrated into functional systems.

- Teams and the communications of which they are comprised:
  - Maintainable communication.
  - Flexible extensible communication.
  - Working communication.
  - Bug free communication.
  - People capable of understanding and working with communication.
  - Communication that delivers critical, valuable and timely functionality.
  - Communication that can be integrated into functional teams.

XP should not be tried unless quality code and honest communications are your outcomes.

Agile stars ✮✮✮✮✮

I give it 5 stars out of 5 as an Agile approach and set of tools because it is the only one I have ever seen, or heard about, delivering and continuing to maintain the benefits of Agile in a software development environment.

It is more concerned with the outcomes of its practices than the details of how they are implemented. It is more interested in how well the software is written than how well XP is implemented. Its techniques are guidelines. If you fully understand what they are delivering and the consequences, you can substitute or omit any of it.

It is neither a process nor a methodology – it is a set of tools that support a pragmatic attitude to software development. Because of this it adapts and evolves with the technologies and businesses it works with.

Many of the tools, simply because they are based on common sense, work in different domains (test first, pairing etc.) but XP makes no claims about anything other than software development. Certain tools such as pair programming and test first can even improve projects in waterfall environments. To get the full Agile benefit it is necessary to make the change in perspective it suggests toward software development and software. Much of it then becomes intuitive and appears to be nothing but good housekeeping and common sense.

A short note on TFP and TDD

There is a subtle difference between Test First programming (TFP) and Test Driven Development (TDD). The terms are often confused and interchanged. In addition the terms are both evolving new meanings depending on the guru in question.

Having two terms for essentially the same thing is unnecessary and provides opportunity for semantic confusion. It can lead to misunderstandings or deliberate attempts to reintroduce "big design up front" by interpreting "test first" or "test driven" as a method of documenting tests, designing a detailed test harness or coding a test suite before development begins.

In both TFP and TDD the tests evolve with the code and the code with the tests.

Test First Programming means that unit tests are coded JUST before every bit of functional code is developed. Just enough code is written to pass each test. You must know what outcome you expect from every bit of code in order to write a test. If you cannot express your intent in a test you do not know what you are doing or why you are doing it.

The tests stay with the code and are run every time the code is integrated. If the purpose or implementation of the code changes so do the tests at the point of change.

Test first development provides you with complete test coverage at a very low level. It provides confidence to build on sound foundations and acts like an alarm system if future changes break the code.

It encourages good design by nudging you toward low coupling and high cohesion and it forces you to examine your understanding of the requirements and what exactly you are doing. By writing the tests in tandem with the code you focus on the purpose of the code and the code becomes self regulating.

Test Driven Development is a bit like TFP with refactoring and acceptance tests added in. It discriminates between the tests written at a low level in the code and a higher order of tests. Requirements are expressed as a set of user acceptance tests. All unit tests must support an acceptance test. If there are implementation problems they can cause both the existing code and the acceptance tests to be questioned and refactored/evolved if necessary.

This is important: Neither of these advocates writing all the tests as a sort of low level design before you begin coding. They are both evolutionary approaches that allow testing to influence code design and implementation. They allow code design and implementation to influence system design.

The Agile Alliance

The Agile manifesto

"We are uncovering better ways of developing software by doing it and helping others do it. Through this work we have come to value:

Individuals and interactions over processes and tools
Working software over comprehensive documentation
Customer collaboration over contract negotiation
Responding to change over following a plan

That is, while there is value in the items on the right, we value the items on the left more."

The Agile principles

Our highest priority is to satisfy the customer through early and continuous delivery of valuable software.

Welcome changing requirements, even late in development. Agile processes harness change for the customer's competitive advantage.

Deliver working software frequently, from a couple of weeks to a couple of months, with a preference to the shorter time-scale.

Business people and developers must work together daily throughout the project.

Build projects around motivated individuals. Give them the environment and support they need, and trust them to get the job done.

The most efficient and effective method of conveying information to and within a development team is face-to-face conversation.

Working software is the primary measure of progress.

Agile processes promote sustainable development. The sponsors, developers, and users should be able to maintain a constant pace indefinitely.

Continuous attention to technical excellence and good design enhances agility.

Simplicity-the art of maximizing the amount of work not done-is essential.

The best architectures, requirements, and designs emerge from self-organizing teams.

At regular intervals, the team reflects on how to become more effective, then tunes and adjusts its behaviour accordingly.

Agile Manifesto (2001) signatories

Extreme Programming
>Kent Beck
>Ward Cunningham
>Ron Jeffries
>Martin Fowler
>James Grenning
>Robert C. Martin

Scrum
>Ken Schwaber
>Jeff Sutherland
>Mike Beedle

DSDM
>Arie van Bennekum

Feature Driven Development
>Jon Kern

Pragmatic Programming
>Dave Thomas
>Andrew Hunt

Adaptive Software Development
>Jim Highsmith

Crystal Methodologies

Alastair Cockburn

Other

Brian Marick (Testing)
Steve Mellor (UML and OO)

Part Three – Software Development Project Models

Waterfalls and Spirals

For purposes of orientation this is a quick look at the evolution of the way software development projects have been managed.

The Waterfall Model

Why it's called waterfall

Everything flows downhill.

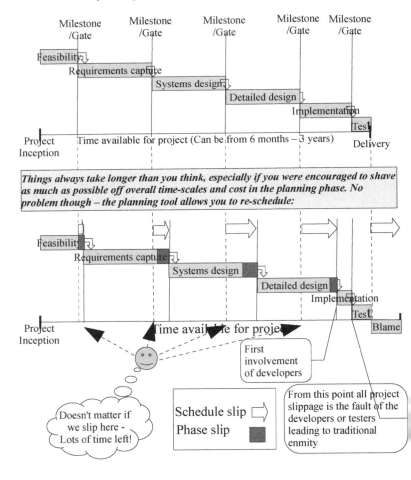

116 | Waterfalls and Spirals

The flaw with waterfall

When Winston Royce presented this model of project management in a paper in 1970 he was using it as an example of a flawed and impossible model. As a result the poor man is often credited with being the inventor of waterfall methodology.

The idea of breaking the project down into discrete phases and completing each phase before starting the next seems to be a good one. Indeed this is a good way to carry out most projects as long as they are not software development projects.

The problem is that it depends on what is known as Big Design Up Front (BDUF). You design things in detail before you build them.

In software development the technology changes so fast that many new projects are unknown territory even if you have experienced people doing them.

In waterfall you do the planning and commitment to time-scales and cost before the requirements capture or the design and certainly the development have been carried out. In practice, although there is much talk of basing costs on estimates, these estimates are either pulled out of thin air or people are told what time they have available and are only asked to schedule the work – i.e. break down the available time between the tasks they think they have to complete. More often than not this is also based on incomplete and incoherent information about the requirements and design.

Each phase is single step (you do it only once) and gated (you cannot start the next phase until the current one is completed and signed off).

When this type of methodology was first mooted (by Herbert T Bennington in 1956) it was suggested that its success depended on the extensive use of prototypes.

In other words the inherent weakness of single step gated approach was recognised right at the outset. The solution was obviously to prototype each phase before you did it so that you could get feedback from the next phase to tell you what it needs the current phase to deliver.

It is almost like having a shadow project running under the actual project.

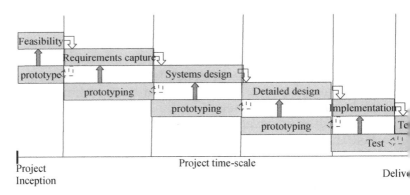

Practitioners of waterfall seem to have either never considered it at all or to have thought that this double dipping would be a waste of time. It seems to have been forgotten that the suggestion had ever even been made.

Given the state of many projects following this model and the obvious remedy suggested in 1956, it was not such a big jump for Barry Boehm in 1986 to suggest the logical step of implementing a spiral model.

The Spiral model

Why it's called spiral

It spirals around phases and uses the feedback from the last one as the input for the next. There are more detailed explanations but the spiral model is essentially this – a series of mini waterfalls with each cycle getting closer to something acceptable to the user. It acknowledges that you really need to go through the whole project at least once before you have any idea what it will involve and how to plan for or design it. It drives out the risks, alternatives and designs as it goes.

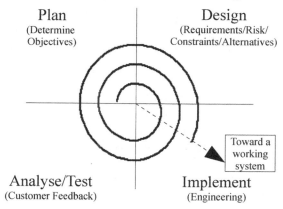

Plan
(Determine
Objectives)

Design
(Requirements/Risk/
Constraints/Alternatives)

Toward a
working
system

Analyse/Test
(Customer Feedback)

Implement
(Engineering)

While this model makes a lot of sense it never really dislodged the waterfall method. Many consider it to be essentially a series of waterfalls. It did, however, provide a launch pad for the iterative and incremental development cycles that underpin all Agile methodologies.

Iterative and incremental cycles

Many people find the PDSA (Plan, do, study, act) approach effective. It recognises that sometimes only by doing it do you know how to do it, what effect doing it is going to have and how much of it to do.

It echoes the scientific method[33] proposed and used by the likes of Francis Bacon and Galileo: hypothesise, experiment and evaluate.

Iterative cycles use this type of approach to focus on the highest priority and incrementally build things one layer at a time relying on real and timely feedback to guide the project to a successful conclusion. Feedback from the previous cycles helps identify risk, determine actual requirements and prioritise action.

Almost all of the Agile methodologies suggest that you work in these iterative cycles. Each cycle includes its own bookends of planning beforehand and evaluation afterwards. The evaluation of this phase becomes the planning of the next.

Each cycle produces a limited but fully functioning system. The advantage is that you have a deliverable system at the end of each cycle.

For new systems this means that you would need a number of cycles before actually delivering the system. On mature systems it means that you potentially drop new and evolving functionality into the live system at the end of every development cycle.

Doing things this way achieves two very valuable outcomes:

---

33 Not to be confused with Scientific Management which was invented for manufacturing in the late 19th and early 20th centuries and provided the world with time and motion studies and decades of inhuman management practices.

1. It identifies projects that are going to fail, early in the process before they have a chance to sap finance and morale.
2. It makes sure that the most important functionality is worked on as early as it can be. That means that if for any reason the project ends prematurely, the best value has been achieved for the investment already made.

These depend on both iterating and incrementing.

It is important to understand the difference between iterations and increments so that you apply them both. Iteration is repeating the same thing in cycles. Incrementing is building on success and real feedback.

You can iterate with short waterfall cycles and while this may improve things you can still miss out on potential benefits and never understand or achieve your outcome. It leads to brittle plans and design that ignores the outcomes of iterations and commits you to actions regardless of real outcomes.

Incrementing is a tool of evolution and provides space to take the best decisions and courses of action as they become clear.

Any approach that leaves out the incremental ingredient by ignoring the physical implementation of the actual outcome can iterate to oblivion quite quickly.

RAD — Rapid Application Development

Rapid Application Development was a similar reaction to the same difficulties that inspired Agile and happened about the same time. James Martin proposed RAD in 1991. It is also iterative but it is not incremental in the same way as Agile.

The main differences between Agile and RAD, and those that confuse many discussions about Agile, are:

1. RAD uses prototyping as its main practice while Agile evolves the system incrementally from prioritised and fully deliverable and improvable features.
2. RAD uses minimal planning while Agile concerns itself largely with planning as an ongoing and evolving activity.
3. RAD is a short sharp effort at the inception of a software system focussed on initial delivery while Agile is an evolutionary approach throughout the life of the system from conception to decommissioning. It involves ongoing analysis, requirements capture, delivery, production, maintenance and, most importantly, change.

Agile develops the system by addressing the highest priority requirements as simply and quickly as possible and then by continuing to evolve and re-factor that system. What you get up front in Agile is not a prototype, it is the core of the eventual system and it should work in production from its first delivery even if at first it only says hello to you and asks you to log in. Agile delivers fully functional, prioritised and restricted, requirements to be delivered onto a working system.

Prototyping

Prototyping is a useful way to demonstrate to clients how the system will look and behave but it tends to confuse them about what is actually delivered and the actual state of the project. Prototypes tend to "fake" functionality, giving stakeholders the impression that the system is closer to delivery than it is and leading them to underestimate the effort involved in delivering the actual functionality. Prototypes are disposable by nature and in RAD each prototype is a new development.

Using RAD

RAD is not Agile but it is a useful technique. Under specific circumstances, on small or start-up developments with stakeholders and users who understand exactly what is going on, it can be an effective way to proceed. There is something to be said for coding prototypes over and over again until you have ironed out all the kinks. Being able to throw away a prototype does free you from mistakes you might have made and allows you to engage with what you know you should have done.

I can even think of circumstances where RAD and Agile could sit well together. XP uses a form of prototyping called spike solutions. These are pretty rare and are used to explore options and solve technical problems bringing knowledge rather than code back to the main project. They are usually very short, time-boxed and have very specific outcomes. I can imagine expanding spike solutions to a RAD for some parts of some systems. It would require a mature customer with well defined requirements that would respond well and benefit from this approach.

Part Four – Observations and Advice

Comparing Scrum and XP

A convenient façade

Scrum sometimes presents the following proposal:

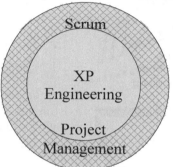

However if you take away the Scrum façade you often find the following reality:

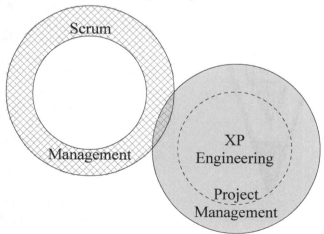

Scrum operates at the existing interface of planning and organisation. It only accepts feedback that relates to time, cost and progress (and compliance to Scrum). As with waterfall it is has nothing to say about the quality aspect of scope nor the production and maintenance issues of code. This makes it attractive to organisations impressed with certification and looking to adopt Agile but not actually wanting to change anything. It can be used as a lightweight planning tool that continues to conceal technical realities from management with the warm fuzzy aspect of Agile.

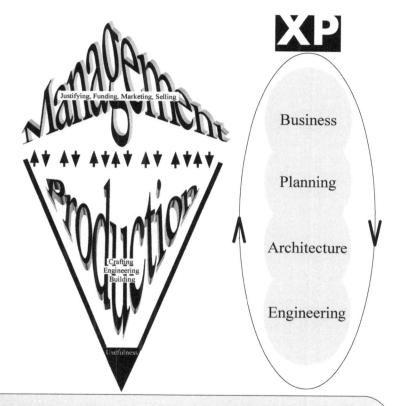

Extreme Programming (XP) spans the interface between management and production. It removes the need for compliance and widens the communication bandwidth between Management and Production by providing a common language and deploying cross functional teams in shared workspaces. It improves the architecture of the code and the system by providing focus and highlighting the value of solid engineering practices and insisting on making managers and developers face some harsh realities through end to end feedback.

Agile shopping list

- Co-Located Teams
- Automated Testing
- Automated Integration
- Version Control
- Decision Makers
- Vision and Commitment
- Generative Learning Environment
- Estimation Skills
- Negotiation Skills
- Creative Environment
- Self Organisation with Direction

Co-Located Teams

Co-located teams – Many Agile people try to fudge this one but it is essential. Agile is about professionals working together in the medium of code and this requires them to put their hands in it together to shape it and have the confidence to change it. It can include people who work from home but are in the office often enough to create relationships with the rest of the team and who can make use of communications technology to do pair working.

Automated Testing

Automated testing tools – be sensible about this. Automation is generally good but big expensive tools can push you back to *"big integration at the end"* behaviour because the tools can easily start driving the process and encourage associated unhelpful behaviours that replace thinking things through.
J-Unit is still the original and best Java unit-test tool. Versions exist for other languages. Mock objects should

also be an essential part of your basic tool-kit. After this I suggest you talk to your test and integration specialists and include them in your development teams.

Automated Integration

Automated integration tools – you need something that can compile and run your code against the unit tests many times a day. It is an essential part of an Agile development environment and will encourage lots of great practices and behaviours.

Version Control

Version control software — if you are not already using it you are a cowboy and I hope the posse catches up with you soon!

Decision Makers

Access to decision makers – there needs to be constant business input. This can be a customer who is prepared to work near or with the team or a proxy customer or product owner. There are decision points every day and quick resolution of these can save the programmers a lot of stress and the project a lot of time and money.

Vision and Commitment

Management commitment and vision – the people managing this need to understand the real cost/benefit of Agile at every level of their organisation and understand what is happening so that they properly interpret the consequences of working this way. There *are* consequences and things will be very different if you have been used to using command and control.

Generative Learning Environment

Time and opportunity to explore and improve technical and interpersonal skills – Software Development is a continuum. Technology advances and you need the programmers to advance with it. New techniques, languages and tools are surfacing all the time and your developers need to know which ones are useful. This means that they get to decide on the tools, languages and environments they use. If you force them to use something because you have got a whole lorry load of it cheap from a nice salesperson, you deserve what you get.

Time to explore and investigate new technology and tools – see above.

Time to consider what is happening in the world at large and how that relates to what you are doing – see above.

Estimation Skills

Universal estimation skills – this is a game for everyone to play. The people doing the work need to make the estimates so that they are not rail-roaded into impossibilities. The people paying for the work need to have some idea of what to budget for and if it is still worth doing based on an informed cost/benefit analysis.

Negotiation Skills

Universal negotiation skills – negotiating is not about arguing or winning it is about finding the highest common denominator and communicating consequences.

Creative Environment

Space to be alone – pair programming and teamwork is all very well but everyone needs time to go noodle about with ideas and get things straight in their own head. A creative environment is one that allows people to think as well as share ideas and learning.

Self Organisation with Direction

Democratic hierarchy – we need people with authority to make decisions/change/declare success/failure to provide this skill as a service to the project team. These decisions need to be requested. Trust me; authority that is invited is far more effective than authority that is imposed. There is a huge difference between self organisation and self direction. The Trousers of Reality:Volume 2 — *Managing Knowledge* discusses this in more detail and, among other things, examines how Agile is related to chaos and to systems theory.

Index

A

B

C

The Trousers
of
Reality

Volume One – Working Life

"unconventional and bold"
- Ian Alexander
(Author of Discovering Requirements)

This is the first volume of an exciting new series. It suggests seeking out and using persistent and tested principles to uncover the ***deep structure underlying reality***. It uses systems engineering as a metaphor for life and looks at some of the principles underlying linguistics, systems thinking, Lean, Agile, complex systems, evolution, education and scientific exploration of the universe. It has been described as:

"a handbook for thinking"

"a self help book for bewildered engineers and others"

"down to earth, practical and very sensible"

"Subversive"

"Inspiring"

"If you have ever been torn between deadlines and burnout, stretched between politics and technology, or simply wondered 'How am I going to get through this?', I think that this book definitely has something to offer you."
- Greg Rolan (IT consultant)

The Trousers
of
Reality
Volume Two – Managing Knowledge

"*dangerously clever*"
- Nicholas Furlong
(Wexford Echo)

The journey into the ***deep structure of reality*** continues with the latest volume in the Trousers of Reality.

It discusses how we create, use and inhabit our own models of the universe in order to survive.

It looks at how we deal with the changes that learning, progress and scientific enquiry force us to apply to our models.

It explores project management as one of those models and how commerce and business are shaping society.

It searches through Neuroplasticity, Chaos Theory, Uncertainty, epistemology, philosophy, the theory of knowledge and explains how Agile, NLP, Theory of Constraints and similar approaches are unconsciously making use of all of these things.

Lightning Source UK Ltd.
Milton Keynes UK
UKOW06f2004060815

256533UK00015B/240/P